# TOO MUCH STUFF

## DE-CLUTTERING YOUR HEART AND HOME

### KATHRYN PORTER

BEACON HILL PRESS
OF KANSAS CITY

ISBN-13: 978-0-8341-2256-7
ISBN-10: 0-8341-2256-1

Printed in the
United States of America

Cover Design: Brandon R. Hill

**Library of Congress Cataloging-in-Publication Data**

Porter, Kathryn, 1971-
  Too much stuff : de-cluttering your heart and home / Kathryn Porter.
    p. cm.
  Includes bibliographical references.
  ISBN 0-8341-2256-1 (pbk.)
    1. Wealth—Religious aspects—Christianity. 2. Materialism—Religious aspects—
Christianity. 3. Stewardship, Christian. 4. Housekeeping. 5. Storage in the home.
I. Title.
BR115.W4P67 2006
241'.68—dc22
                              2006003194

10  9  8  7  6  5  4  3  2

# CONTENTS

# PROLOGUE

## THE ULTIMATE COST OF CLUTTER

"LET me not destroy the beauty of today by grieving over yesterday . . . or worrying about tomorrow. May I cherish and appreciate my shell collection each and every day . . . for I know not when the tide will come and wash my treasures away."[1]

## GOING HOME

"She was such a wonderful person."

"We are really going to miss her at work."

"She was such a good friend."

"I can't believe she's gone."

"She was too young to leave us this soon."

These are just a few of the comments made by those who knew my mother. Only a few months earlier, I had traveled to New York for a baby shower my mother and sister threw for me. Now, I had returned for Mother's funeral.

"I am so sorry about your mother. How did it happen?" people asked.

The paramedics had to push aside boxes and bags of junk to clear a path so they could get the stretcher through the house. There was too much stuff.

Boxes, bags, trash, and debris were everywhere, three to four feet high in many places. A narrow pathway carved a trail from the front door to the couch that became my mother's deathbed. A layer of vomit lined the clutter by the couch.

"Complications of diabetes," I replied. *Yet in my heart I knew collecting too much stuff contributed to her early death. But how do you tell someone your mother was suffocated by a house filled with waist-high clutter?*

This was our little secret. We couldn't share our grief, lest others learn the truth.

## A HISTORY LESSON

My mother wasn't always that way. When we were young, she kept a messy house, but never so extreme. Back then, only a single layer of clutter decorated the living room floor. Just a few giant piles of laundry lounged on the couches—as well as the recliner, the coffee table, and almost everything else with a flat surface. We didn't have stacks of boxes everywhere in the house—most stayed hidden in my parents' bedroom.

As time passed, bags of gifts and bargains were added to the mounds of folded clothes scattered across the house. Every week, my mother brought home a box or bag of stuff, maybe thinking no one would notice. She had a reputation as a giving person and was known for her bargain-hunting talent. A plethora of gift items littered our home along with clearance merchandise that she *might* use someday. Through the years, the piles continued to build up.

The clutter progression peaked with the death of my grandmother. It was no longer just store purchases but boxes full of my grandma's stuff. My mother loved her mother and could not bear to part with her things: Thirty-year-old perfumes that had lost their scent; expired prescription bottles, some with pills in them; old Christmas cards and yellowed stationery; tattered towels and stained tablecloths; even my grandmother's dentures. Mother kept it all.

We tried to help her. We attempted interventions. She stubbornly refused.

## FAMILY TIES

The clutter took its toll on my parents' marriage. They seemed unhappy for a long time, but they were committed to stay together. In my mother's last days, my father remained by her side almost the entire time.

My mother loved her children dearly, but I don't think we ever fully felt the depth of her love in our messy house. Clutter kills. It diminishes, even destroys, relationships.

The mess affected us in different ways. My baby brother was born with a learning disability. Unclear exactly how the clutter impacted their relationship, I recollect behavioral issues that arose when the house was at its messiest. Still, in his childish innocence, he expressed deep love for our mother.

My younger sister visited or talked with our mother almost every day. They had their share of fights, but she loved Mother fiercely.

My other brother harbored feelings of anger toward Mother. Their relationship became estranged.

I resented her for allowing us to grow up in a home we were ashamed of. But as hard as it was to love her, it was impossible not to love her.

□ □ □

"We've got a code blue! Code blue!"

"What's happening?" my sister Pam yelled as she ran toward the double doors leading into the ICU. She grabbed a nurse walking by. "Is it my mother?"

We were told we could not see her—the doctors were working on her. The same response they had been giving us all night.

"Oh no!" Pam sobbed, "It's her . . . I know it's her! I want to see my mother!"

She barreled through the double doors into the ICU, calling for our mother. Hospital staff grabbed her elbows. Her feet and knees dragged on the shiny floor as they escorted her back to us. She begged them to let go, pleading to see our mother. I reached for Pam as she struggled to free herself from their grip.

Crying, she fell toward the floor as I held onto her. She let out another wail, then her body went limp. Helpless and distraught, she collapsed into my arms as she sensed our mother's passing.

□ □ □

## LIKE MOTHER, LIKE DAUGHTER

I loved Mother, but I did not want to be like her. I was proud I wasn't like her. Until I began to sort through her things.

Uncashed payroll checks. Envelopes saved for their return addresses. Bins of gift items. Lost cash. Old purses filled with money and papers. Clothes with the tags still on them.

I began to realize there were habits I had picked up from her. I had de-cluttered a lot in my own home, but I realized where I was headed if I didn't continue making changes in my behavior.

I lost personal and payroll checks. I saved cards to transfer addresses to my Daytimer. I bought gifts throughout the year and stored them in bins. I tended to lose money. I often bought a new purse because the task of cleaning out my current one was too daunting. Unworn clothes I planned to wear someday hung in the closet with the price tags still attached.

I am my mother's daughter.

## CLEANING WITH DAD

My father and I spent countless hours going through folders, mail, and various papers. Our mourning consisted of sifting through clutter in a quiet, lonely house. Although filled with mountains of stuff, each room felt eerie and empty, devoid of life.

We worked our way through at least 50 large office boxes stuffed with manila envelopes and folders. Each envelope contained varying combinations of coupons, napkins, recipes, and cash. Some envelopes were empty. Others held newspaper articles, unused stamps, or wrappers. Most were stashed with coupons and recipes with an occasional savings bond here and there. We had to check every one because we didn't know which ones might be hiding money.

Over the course of more than a month, we sat in silence each day opening piles of envelopes, searching for valuables left behind. We found expired coupons dating back more than 15 years. There were savings bonds my mother never told my father about, Christmas cards written but never sent, recipes and directions to craft projects she saved for future use.

The number of coupons and recipes was staggering. I thanked God my sister Pam didn't experience the mind-numbing affects of this glimpse into my mother's life.

A couple of weeks after I returned home to Colorado, I received a phone call from Pam.

"Kat? You won't believe this. I've been going through a couple of boxes Mom left at my house. It was nothing but envelope after envelope full of recipes and coupons."

"I know, Pam."

"You know?" inquired the quivering voice. "Is that what you and Dad were doing all that time?"

## THE ULTIMATE COST OF CLUTTER

I truly believe my mother's love for things contributed to her early death. She collected stuff she thought she could use someday: Recipes to bake for us, craft projects to make for us, coupons to save us money, gifts to give us. Yet the best gift she could have given us was more time with her. Time we were robbed of—moments of her life the clutter stole.

The cause of death was officially ketoacidosis, a condition that can occur when a diabetic does not follow the proper medical care. As the clutter increased, my mother stopped taking her medications. It appeared she tried to take them, but then gave up because they were constantly lost in the clutter. I found prescriptions that had never been filled in the boxes and bags she had buried all around the house.

In the end, her possessions owned her. They required her constant attention. Physically, she could not keep up with them. Mentally, she must have been terribly burdened. And in the end, much of what she held so dear was donated to the Salvation Army or left in front of the house for trash pickup.

□ □ □

I rushed from the airport to the hospital just a couple of hours before my mother passed away. I waited to see her until the doctors finally cleared us for our last visit. The morphine that eased her excruciating pain sedated her into unconsciousness. Only her spirit knew of my presence.

Although she could not hear us, we said our good-byes. The

EKG readings slowed to a flat line as her weak, tired body gave up.

She was only 57 years old.

□ □ □

### HOMEBUILDING

*"For I know the plans I have for you," declares the* LORD, *"plans to prosper you and not to harm you, plans to give you hope and a future"* (Jer. 29:11).

The bittersweet story of my mother's struggle with clutter does not have to be your story. God has great plans for you. He loves you through all the messes you make in life, and not just the ones involving clutter. He knows you're not perfect, yet He still desires a prominent place in your life.

Do not be discouraged. For when God is our hope, we know we have a future.

### De-Cluttering My Heart

Lord, forgive me for: (*This prayer point is for clearing your conscience. Confess what is on your mind.*)

Lord, thank You for: (*This prayer point is for acknowledging God's blessing. Develop a thankful heart by finding things to be thankful for and sharing your gratitude.*)

Lord, help me with: (*This prayer point is for asking God's help in specific areas. Recognize that God will show His strength through your weakness.*)

### De-Cluttering My Home

How does clutter impair my lifestyle? Do I lose things? Do I spend extra money buying items I already have? Think of specific examples.

What would I do if an unexpected guest knocked on my front door? Would I invite my guest inside? Or would I just happen to be on my way out the door and politely excuse myself?

How has the too-much-stuff lifestyle affected my relationships? What would I like to change?

# 1 MY STORY

**"CLUTTER** can indeed be traced back to Adam, who, when his fig leaves were worn out and should have been discarded, pressed and saved them as a memory of bygone days."[2]

## IN THE BEGINNING

Some people say that you are born with it—that ability to be tidy housekeepers. I don't believe we're born with an innate talent to clean or that there are "neat freak" and "messy" genes. So where does it start? I can only tell you where it started with me.

I am an example that children learn more by what is caught than what is taught. Although my parents taught me to clean, I caught the behaviors that invite clutter—like saving all kinds of stuff and buying more than I need. I am inclined to stockpile and form emotional attachments to trivial things. I can also see that some of my childhood games may have developed into adult habits.

## GAMES KIDS PLAY

Babies like to play "drop it." You know the game. Baby drops the food or toys on the floor. Mommy (or any adult) picks it up and gives it back to baby. Tiny hands drop it again for Mommy to pick up. I imagine this was my favorite game as a baby, but I'm not so fond of it now that I'm a mommy.

Envision the toddler who enjoys playing "empty it." Little hands explore junk drawers and fling pencils, screws, plastic thingamajigs, old mail, and every last piece of whatever is jammed in there. I was that adorable toddler making this not-so-cute mess. And how about those bookshelves? There's no better fun than emptying all those shelves of books, videos, knickknacks, and decor. My parents' home had lots of shelves. Need I say more? Oh, and don't forget about the clothes in the laundry basket. Whether the clothes are clean or dirty, what a fun mess-making game. Small hands enjoy testing boundaries with these and other versions of "empty it." (My toddler mastered this game fast, but it took a little longer to learn "put it back.")

Preschoolers graduate to what I call "leave it." Children this age like to play with their own toys. They make a mess and leave it for someone else to deal with.

My nieces invited me to play this game, but they don't enjoy it anymore because I changed the rules. I told them that if they care so little about their toys as to leave them lying around, then Aunt Katie will throw them out. The astonishment reflected on those little faces was priceless. This may sound mean, but they owned nearly enough playthings to fill Toys-R-Us.

Another time when my nieces wanted to play "leave it," I took a kinder, gentler approach. I taught them that the more toys they had, the more they had to pick up. I shared that more toys meant more cleaning. Suddenly, they were eager to find toys they no longer loved and donate them to charity. I wish I had learned this lesson when I was their age.

Without setting boundaries on the number of toys and expectations to pick them up, endearing preschoolers may very well play "leave it" right into their teenage years. Worse yet, this could be ingrained as a character trait that will follow them into adulthood. Combined with the proclivity to accumulate more stuff without getting rid of some of the things they already own, they have a recipe for disaster.

## A GROWN-UP STRUGGLE

In the past, I left dirty dishes in the sink. More often than I like to admit, I ignored piles of laundry pleading to be washed. If books, boxes, or bags littered the floor, "leave it" was my motto.

But not putting things away was only part of my problem. The older I got, the more stuff I accumulated. And I seldom parted with any of it.

I had every intention of going through everything and putting it all in order. But there was too much stuff to sort. Too much stuff to organize. I was trapped by the behaviors I caught growing up. I amassed scads of hobby items, clothing, linens, dishes. I accumulated junk mail, old bills, cards, and coupons. I boxed up and stored old clutter to make room for new stuff.

Subsequently, I lacked confidence in my cleaning skills. It wasn't that I didn't know how to wipe down a counter. The problem was, I couldn't find the countertop. I knew how to clear the floor to vacuum, but I was clueless about how to keep all that stuff from creeping back.

I didn't want to be like this. I didn't like living this way. But I didn't know how to change. Why did it appear so easy for others to keep beautiful homes? What was I doing wrong?

Having a presentable home seemed like an impossible dream, yet I knew it was possible because other people did it. I read every book on organizing and cleaning I could get my hands on. I enlisted the help of friends and family whenever possible. I tried several different cleaning systems—index cards, timers, charts and incentives, schedules—just about every method I heard about. But for all my efforts, my best achievements were only temporary fixes.

## A LITTLE BIT OF PRAYER

Initially, I didn't think about seeking God in my struggle. I mean, what does God have to do with cleaning house? It wasn't like He would snap His fingers up in heaven to miraculously transform my messy surroundings into a sparkling, clutter-free home. Sure, I offered some halfhearted prayer attempts in the past. You know, the kind when you're approaching a traffic light on the way to work and you say, "Please, Lord, make the light stay green." But I tried everything else, so I figured it couldn't hurt if I started to seriously pray about it.

I prayed. And prayed. And prayed some more. All the while, the clutter just kept breeding. Then I waited. And continued waiting while praying, wondering why my prayers weren't being answered.

God heard my cry for help with housekeeping skills, but He responded in His timing. Though He didn't answer me overnight, He still answered. And it was not the answer I expected.

## PERSEVERANCE PAYS OFF

I eventually met Holly and Jan at church. Both had a reputation for keeping beautiful homes, so I asked for their help. When they came to my home, I saw that it was difficult for them to understand how I could not know how to keep a clean house. Holly made a comment about all the clutter. Clutter? What clutter? It was my stuff. And my things just needed a home. The issue was my cleaning and organizing, not my stuff. Right? Wrong!

I decided to take a new approach. These women seemed to know about clutter, so I asked them to teach me as if they were teaching a child. I told them to think of me as a four-year-old who didn't know anything about housekeeping. Somewhat startled by my request, they complied. So there I was, a college-educated professional being taught the fundamentals of cleaning as one would teach a preschooler. I earned a master's degree in special education, and now Jan and Holly were giving me one.

## YOU CAN'T KEEP IT ALL!

"You can't keep everything and keep a clean house." Those words, spoken ever so casually, changed my life.

Jan helped me clean the bathroom closet. She stared at the shelves packed with soaps, lotions, candles, pictures, and knick-knacks. "Why are you keeping all this?" she asked.

"A lot of these were gifts. I don't know what to do with them," I said.

"If you are not using them, then why are you keeping them?"

"I don't know. I guess because they were given to me. I can't just throw all these things out. It would be rude. If people found out I threw away their gifts, it might hurt their feelings," I replied. Then I wondered if it might be OK to toss away presents.

Continuing to find more unused, unopened items, she gently prodded, "Well, what are you saving all this stuff for?"

"I don't know. I thought I'd find a use for them someday. I might meet someone who could use them. Maybe someday I can actually use them."

"Well, can we either throw these out or give them to charity? *You can't keep everything and keep a clean house.*"

It was like hearing the magic words. *You can't keep everything and keep a clean house.* Wow! I never thought of it that way. These words made my elusive dream suddenly reachable. It was the answer I'd prayed for.

## QUESTIONS, QUESTIONS, AND MORE QUESTIONS

It didn't occur to me that it was OK to get rid of nice gift items. After all, I watched my great-grandmother, my grand-mother, and my mother save everything—including gifts they didn't use—along with the boxes, the wrapping paper, the rib-bon, and the tissue.

My curiosity took over. What else could I get rid of? How do I decide what to keep? What other things have I been holding on to that I really don't need?

I talked to my friends who kept beautiful homes. Instead of asking for help with cleaning or organizing, I asked them about their methods of handling clutter. How do they keep their homes free of so much stuff? What do they do with possessions they used to love but have outgrown? What happens to expen-sive items they no longer use?

I compared my habits to theirs. Do they keep duplicates? How many bath towels do they own? How many sets of sheets do they own for each bed? What about extra blankets? Are there items they stock up on? What types of keepsakes do they save?

I thought about all the clothes stuffed in dresser drawers and crammed in closets. I always had piles of laundry—clean or dirty—because I didn't have enough room for it all.

How many pairs of jeans do I really need? What about T-shirts and sweatshirts? Do I need all that I have? What don't I wear anymore? Are there clothes that don't fit right or don't complement my figure? What do I have that I just don't like? Am I hanging on to clothes that are torn, faded, or missing buttons? If so, why am I keeping them?

*You can't keep everything and keep a clean house.* What a revelation! I was overcome by a sense of joy and relief. Although this commonsense statement is a simple, obvious fact, it was not obvious to me. No matter how many books I read, how many people tried to help me, or how many cleaning strategies I attempted, the clutter was always in the way. I simply had too much stuff. To learn it, I had to hear it: You can't keep everything and keep a clean house.

I didn't know that having all this stuff was preventing me from having the home I always desired. I am greatly indebted to Holly and Jan for teaching me what I so desperately needed to learn.

## A NEW DIRECTION

Now that I've found the answers, I want to share them with you. You can experience the same joy I've found.

With every piece of clutter that went out the door, I lost pounds of emotional weight. My soul felt lighter. Whatever feelings of comfort or happiness I derived from having too much stuff were multiplied by letting things go. I came to understand a new definition of the word *freedom.* My heart sensed God's presence like never before. And I experienced a peace and clarity previously unknown to me.

Join me by taking the first step in embracing what may be a new philosophy for you.

Write it down. Memorize it. Say it to yourself when you're cleaning. *I can't keep everything and keep a clean house.*

You're on your way!

### HOMEBUILDING

*By wisdom a house is built, and through understanding it is established; through knowledge its rooms are filled with rare and beautiful treasures* (Prov. 24:3-4).

The first step in maintaining a clean house is obtaining the wisdom in how to do it. Nearly anyone can keep a clean house for a day. But *every* day is a different matter. We must seek understanding in how to permanently transform our cluttered rooms into blessing rooms.

Consider that the most beautiful treasures filling our homes are not our possessions, but the people who live with us.

## De-Cluttering My Heart

Lord, forgive me for:

Lord, thank You for:

Lord, help me with:

## De-Cluttering My Home

Do I still play "drop it" and "leave it"? What childhood habits do I need to change? What behaviors can I replace them with?

Am I open to paring down any of my collections? What items am I willing to consider letting go?

Which do I desire more—to keep everything I own or to keep a clean house?

# 2 FIRST THINGS FIRST: DEFINE CLUTTER

**"DOES** your home say 'Come in!' or 'Abandon hope, all ye who enter here?'"[3]

It's true—we can't keep everything and keep a clean house. But how do we decide what to keep? How do we decide what's meaningful in all the clutter?

Until friends gently pointed it out to me, I never knew so much of what I pictured as valuable amounted to nothing more than junk. To develop a deeper understanding, I created expanded definitions for this foe called clutter.

## KNOW YOUR ENEMY

What is clutter? You will get different answers from different people. What holds value and utility to one person can hold the opposite to another. I would tell you that my husband's collection of Hot Wheels Monster Trucks is nothing but clutter. He will tell you that it is of great value to him because he is a monster truck enthusiast and enjoys the thrill of the hunt to locate every model ever made. Who is right? We both are! However, some things are defined as clutter no matter who you ask. For instance, anyone should tell you that the McDonald's bag with the used burger wrapper setting on your kitchen table is clutter.

- ☐ Trash: Yes, one person's trash can be another person's treasure, but there are some things that are just plain trash.

- □ Unorganized things: Be careful. Even organized things amount to clutter if you don't use them.
- □ Unfinished projects: I mean projects you have given up on. If you haven't worked on it in more than a year, it is an unfinished project.
- □ Homeless things: Good things become clutter when they are haphazardly strewn about.
- □ Unused goodies: Consider frequency of use as well. You may want to keep the Christmas tree you use every year, but rethink the bicycle you haven't ridden since college.
- □ Unnecessary duplicates: Do you really need the extra blender?
- □ Visually displeasing objects: Why keep something you think is ugly? But be careful on this one. You may not like your kitchen table, but if it's the only one you have, it's not clutter.
- □ Broken items: If that coffeemaker doesn't work, then toss it and buy a new one.
- □ Clothes that don't fit: How long have you been holding on to those jeans in case you can ever squeeze into them again?
- □ Outdated or obsolete things: Still using a pre-Pentium computer? If it does the job, fine. Just don't keep it as a paperweight because you paid $4,000 for something that today you can't even give away.
- □ Too much of anything: Do you really need 50 pairs of socks? The less you have, the less you have to clean!

Did you ever think there could be so many definitions for clutter? Becoming familiar with them makes it easier to say good-bye to our stuffaholic tendencies. To free ourselves from the things that enslave us to extra and unnecessary housework, we first need to recognize these collections around our home for what they are—clutter.

But clutter goes beyond those things invading our homes. It also steals space in our hearts. There is a psychological realm where collections of bad feelings and negative emotions dwell inside us, cluttering our hearts.

Let's think about this. Physical clutter is what the name implies, the stuff around us that we can see and touch. My clutter-bug friend Katie describes the look of physical clutter in her home. "Every time I walk through the front door, the first thought that runs through my mind is 'Oh, no! We've been robbed!'" Really, it's just too much stuff lying around on her living room floor.

Psychological clutter is emotional heaviness that resides in our hearts. These weights are not tangible, but nonetheless they trouble our souls. What does the psychological clutter look like in your heart?

That which we possess and that which we desire to possess also clutters our hearts. We think, worry, and dream about these things. When it comes to the stuff we own, protecting it, insuring it, maintaining it, storing it, and cleaning it resides in the back of our minds. Even if we're not actively thinking about it, it weighs on us, stealing the room in our hearts once reserved for loved ones and for God.

Do a mental inventory of your home. In your mind, walk through each room in your house. What types of clutter do you see? As you read over the following list, think of the items in your home that you can add to each example.

- ☐ Paper (junk mail, napkins, books)
- ☐ Clothes (items that are outdated, too tight, stained, or torn)
- ☐ Toys (broken, unsafe, old, or unused playthings)
- ☐ Gadgets (high maintenance devices, seldom used appliances)
- ☐ Kitchenware (excessive pans, chipped dishes, dusty mugs)
- ☐ Technology (spam, floppy disks, CDs)
- ☐ Food (expired or moldy "tasty" treats)
- ☐ Plastics (grocery bags, butter containers)
- ☐ Outdoor stuff (weeds, junk car)
- ☐ Pet supplies (chewed up collars, cat litter on the floor)
- ☐ Decorative items (knickknacks, wall hangings, furniture with no purpose)
- ☐ Holiday items (gifts, wrapping paper, cards, decorations)

□ Grooming supplies (dull razors, perfume that lost its scent, old makeup)
□ Inherited things (someone else's stuff passed on to you)

What kinds of psychological clutter do you want to let go of?

□ Heart "problems" (any range of negative emotions—bitterness, anger, envy, worry, pride)
□ Unhealthy relationships (the emotional drain felt from tending relationships with people who use you without giving back or from trying to maintain close friendships with too many people; codependency)
□ Anxiety (the pressure felt due to possession overload, debt overload, or activity overload; anything causing feelings of burnout; that which causes feelings of being overwhelmed or helpless)

## OH, BEHAVE!

Now, let's take a look at how our actions—the use of our own free will—invite clutter into our lives. Clutter does not walk into our homes by itself. How we behave is directly related to how much stuff we bring through our front doors. Our attitudes and behaviors produce a *too-much-stuff* lifestyle.

Let's consider what we welcome into our lives and the behaviors we need to change to stop the flow of this insidious enemy.

**Sentimental Clutter** (items you keep because of emotional attachment to a specific event or season in life)

Some of my friends who are moms find it especially difficult to toss old baby clothes. It's one thing to keep a few favorite outfits. It's another to keep everything your baby ever wore. My husband threw a fit the first time I tried to throw out his old, shoddy gym shorts from high school. After recognizing he retained mementos of far greater value from that time in his life, he finally agreed to say good-bye to the shorts. I struggled with letting go of cards and letters—until I experienced the joy of decluttering. By not holding on so tightly to every scribble from the past, I made room to live to the fullest in the present.

**Inherited Clutter** (anything you keep because it was passed down to you)

When my great-grandfather passed away, my grandmother had trouble throwing away anything with his handwriting on it. She held on to the ugliest mementos just because he owned them. Likewise, my mother kept my grandmother's old hair rollers and useless gadgets. Not everything is an heirloom. We have a choice: we can leave our children with a legacy rich in memories or a legacy defaced by clutter. Let's honor our loved ones who are no longer with us by cherishing their memories rather than enshrining their belongings. Share funny stories. Laugh about the good times. Remember the love.

**Vanity Clutter** (things you buy to impress your friends, keeping-up-with-the-Jones's purchases, luxury items)

When I bought my first house, I based my definition of necessities on what other people owned. I thought we needed a guest bedroom because almost everyone I knew had one. Pure vanity. We purchased a three-bedroom home, and we didn't even have any kids. Until our baby was born, those extra rooms became storage areas. We foolishly embraced higher mortgage payments on a bigger house so we could have more space to store stuff. Vanity causes clutter and costs money.

**Samaritan Clutter** (items you keep to help others someday)

While going through the garage, I asked my husband why he needed so many drills. Why have a cordless drill and one with a cord? Why do we need three of each in varying wattage? He had an answer for everything, but one response blew me away. "Honey, a neighbor might need to borrow a drill someday. I don't want to lend out my good ones." Ugggh! So we are keeping tools that amount to clutter so we can be good neighbors? We finally agreed that it's OK to say no and place boundaries on lending practices. We won't lend anything we can't afford to replace if someone else breaks it or fails to return it. Of course, we want to be Good Samaritans by helping others, but that doesn't mean keeping things we truly don't need.

**"Just in Case" Clutter** (things you hold on to just in case you ever need them)

Why did I keep all those clothes from college that no longer fit? So if I lost weight I would have something to wear. Did you do that? And guess why I kept five muffin pans. Someday, I might want to bake muffins—a lot of them.

**"OPP" Clutter** (Other People's Property that you either borrowed or are storing upon request)

At one point, my willingness to store things for friends hindered my de-cluttering efforts. When we say no to storing other people's stuff, we say yes to a clean home for us. And the same goes for borrowed items too.

**Clearance Clutter** (things you buy only because they are on sale or a good deal)

Who doesn't love a good sale? To clutterbugs, bargains, close-outs, flea markets, thrift stores, and yard sales are like bars and taverns to the alcoholic. Instead of liquor, our drug of choice is stuff. Let's minimize visits to places that tempt us to bring home more clutter.

**Financial Clutter** (taking on debt)

Credit cards. Buy now, pay later. I've read that we spend as much as 18 percent more money when we use plastic. So we buy more stuff we don't need or can't afford and then get more bills in the mail. What a deal!

**Activity Clutter** (overscheduling your calendar, participating in too many hobbies)

It's hard to keep a clean house when we lead such busy lives. With the advent of supersized meals, we apparently also embraced supersized calendars. The problem is that no matter how large a daily calendar we purchase, there are still only 24 hours in one day. Maybe we should reexamine the activities in which we participate. How often do we complain that we're too tired to keep up with our household chores? How many of us miss out on our families because of the busyness that captivates our attention? Take a second look at what you say yes to. It's time to make room for investing in our homes, our families, and quiet time with God.

**Conversational Clutter** (gossip, profanity)

Who says clutter can't spew from our mouths? Women, in particular, need to watch for this as we tend to talk more than men. But what do we talk about? Is it encouraging? Uplifting? Noble? Praiseworthy? Or is it laced with put-downs and negativity? We are told, "For out of the overflow of the heart the mouth speaks" (Matt. 12:34). What do your words and tone of voice say about your heart? One of my favorite Bible verses (Eph. 4:29) says, "Do not let any unwholesome talk come out of your mouths, but only what is helpful for building others up according to their needs, that it may benefit those who listen." In my book, if our words don't meet this command, we are talking trash. And we all know that trash is another form of clutter.

**Intellectual Clutter** (addiction to news, facts, trivia)

My baby brother is a sports fanatic, memorizing stats and scores. My husband spends hours on the computer surfing sites about Unimogs and trucks. I am a Fox News junkie. What is your addiction? Are you obsessed with the stock market? Do you know the words to every song recorded by your favorite singer? Can you repeat lines from movies on cue? And what about the slogans and jingles from watching so many commercials? Beware of information overload. We don't want clutter in our homes, nor do we desire it in our hearts and minds.

## THE JOURNEY

Think you know clutter yet? Congratulations! Now you will have a better idea of what to keep and what to toss. It's a long road ahead, but it's exciting and worth the sacrifice of letting go of possessions we once gripped tightly.

Be prepared as you continue on this marvelous journey. It

will change your life. By clearing out the clutter, you make room for countless blessings in your life. Blessings like improved relationships, increased energy levels, less stress, better health, decreased debt, peace of mind, and a house that is more than a building to hold stuff, but a place that truly feels like home. Be ready to experience the joy of de-cluttering and a home that you can keep clean.

### HOMEBUILDING

*Do not store up for yourselves treasures on earth, where moth and rust destroy, and where thieves break in and steal. But store up for yourselves treasures in heaven, where moth and rust do not destroy, and where thieves do not break in and steal. For where your treasure is, there your heart will be also* (Matt. 6:19-21).

Moths create unsightly holes in our linens. Rust corrodes our pots, hammers, appliances, and other metal objects. Thieves swipe our money and our belongings. So what does that leave us? Treasures in heaven. These do not fade or break. They cannot be stolen. Time does not erode them.

What are eternal treasures? These are treasures of the heart. They consist of things like loving relationships, acts of kindness, grace, and forgiveness. Let's remember our most priceless treasure, the pearl of great price, our salvation through Jesus. Let's not bury that pearl in a heart cluttered with pride and attachment to earthly treasures.

### De-Cluttering My Heart

Lord, forgive me for:

Lord, thank You for:

Lord, help me with:

## De-Cluttering My Home

What are some new insights I have learned by exploring the definitions and types of clutter?

What types of clutter are most prevalent in my home? In my heart?

What benefits do I anticipate from de-cluttering?

# 3 BECOME AN OLYMPIC DE-CLUTTERER

**"WHEN** you make yourself at home, you surround yourself with the people you love, the objects you cherish, the memories that warm you, and the ideas that motivate you. You work to create a nest that helps you to be happy and productive, an environment that rests and renews you. You choose to invest your time, your care, your loving energy to keep your nest clean and warm and welcoming."[4]

De-cluttering is a marathon, not a sprint. Like a runner in training, we practice de-cluttering every day to reach our destination—a presentable-looking home. Except our marathon begins anew each day. There is always something to be cleaned or clutter needing to be tossed. When the big mess is gone, the marathons become smaller and easier until they feel like short sprints. What once wore us out now becomes a walk in the park. So how do you get there? Train to be an Olympic-class de-clutterer by practicing the five keys to successful de-cluttering.

## KEY 1: SIGN UP FOR THE RACE

Join the race. Take a proactive stance against clutter. Set the pace and lead others by example.

Don't wait for someone else to start running. Stop being a bystander. Don't sit there and tolerate the mess. Step up to the starting line even if other family members don't share your desire to run, much less cheer you on.

*Get on your mark.* Take measures to stop the influx of clutter, such as removing your name from mailing lists. Stop it at the door before it even makes it into the house.

*Get set.* Assess the clutter residing in your home. Decide to part with some of your belongings.

*Go!* Make the first move. Start running. Throw that clutter out!

Here are some examples of how I run in the de-cluttering marathon:

□ My husband leaves a screwdriver, glue, gloves, and some miscellaneous items on the floor. I put them in a box and mark it *Charity*. I lovingly tell him that if it's important enough to keep, then it's important enough to put away. He now knows to put it away or check the Charity box. (I call this tough love!)

□ My child leaves his toys everywhere. He is too young to care about picking them up and putting them away. Therefore, until he learns to pick up his messes, I place limits on how many toys he is allowed to have out at the same time.

□ A friend has some clothes she no longer wants. She asks me if I'd like them. I have enough clothes, so I politely decline her offer.

□ I'm at the mall and a salesperson hands me a flyer. I say, "No, thank you," because I know it will clutter my purse. And who knows when I will get around to cleaning that out again?

□ There is a *big* sale at my favorite department store. I decide not to go because I know I'll probably end up buying something I don't need that will end up cluttering my home.

## KEY 2: KEEP YOUR EYES ON THE FINISH LINE

How do you envision the finish? To help clarify your vision, let's break this into three parts—the look, the feel, and the function.

## The Look

Other than clean, how would you like your home to look? What kind of furniture do you want? What types of decor do you find attractive? How will you fill or leave open the space in your home? What do you see in the small but significant details of your home?

After growing up in a house where taking a design risk meant painting the walls off-white, I love experimenting with color. I want my home to look colorful and coordinated with vibrant yet soothing tones. I like simple styles with touches of elegance. Rather than purchasing furniture piecemeal, I prefer a matching set.

I envision a low-maintenance, streamlined design. For me, those small details involve finding easy-to-clean fixtures and decor. For instance, I once thought intricately carved book-shelves were beautiful. Now that I know about the extra elbow grease it takes to clean them, this type of furniture has lost its charm. I see the intricate carvings as crevices to snugly hold debris. More dirt, more dust, more clutter. No thanks.

Instead of selecting decor based solely on aesthetics or cost, I ask the following:

- □ Do I really love it?
- □ Is it a want or a need?
- □ Does it fit the theme of the room?
- □ Is it difficult to clean?
- □ How costly is it to maintain?
- □ Is it so trendy that it will be outdated in just a few years?
- □ Will it attract clutter?

## The Feel

What kind of atmosphere do you desire for your home? How does your home make you feel when you walk through the front door? Does it feel like a dog pound? A hospital? A rock concert? A boxing ring? Colors, scents, sounds, communication styles, and even our personal values influence the feel of our homes.

I want my home to feel like my sanctuary. When I walk through the doorway, I envision a place that emanates serenity —a haven to rest and rejuvenate where I take shelter from the disorder of the outside world. A quiet refuge of happy noise where I experience the love and laughter of family.

How does your home make you feel? Warm and peaceful? Chaotic and tense? Is your home a retreat or just a building you happen to sleep in?

How can we create sanctuaries for our families? Here are a few ideas:

- ☐ Limit music to songs with positive messages.
- ☐ Venture toward colors—warm and peaceful or cool and soothing—that make you feel happy.
- ☐ Burn vanilla or fruit-scented candles.
- ☐ Greet family members with love, encouragement, acceptance, and patience.
- ☐ Express appreciation for one another.
- ☐ Build an environment of emotional safety by reserving judgment.
- ☐ Focus on the good and avoid stewing over faults.
- ☐ Provide gentle guidance with humility and respect.
- ☐ Pray together.
- ☐ And get rid of the clutter.

## The Function

What is the purpose of your home? Does it serve as only a place to eat and sleep? What do you want to use your home for?

I once dreamed of having a beautiful home for entertaining guests. Scads of specialty dishes and party supplies sat topped with dust, even on those rare occasions when I hosted a party. I bought extra bedding, towels, and sundries, not to mention the furnishings and decorations, for a cluttered room guests rarely used.

To meet the needs of others, we flexed our schedule and stretched our home. Our house became a storage unit not just for our possessions but also for other people's property. Instead of hosting friends for dinner, we entertained their stuff. With helper hearts and poor boundaries, my husband and I lived by an unspoken door-is-always-open philosophy. Friends and family knew they could stay with us anytime they needed shelter, preferring the pullout couch over the cluttered guest room!

Our desire to help others took us offtrack and set us back in our attempts to create a presentable home. Like a runner who leaps off the track to tie someone's shoelace in the bleachers, we sabotaged our efforts in our race to de-clutter.

With no vision for the function of our home, we gave in to competing priorities that put our own family in second place. Then a friend gave me the wise counsel I needed to determine if I wanted my home for nesting or community service.

I realized that God wanted me to put my family first. It's not about choosing family to the exclusion of serving others. I can still be a friend without sacrificing my home.

When I chose nesting, I placed priority on building my family and strengthening my marriage. Nesting means the primary function of my home is to nurture family relationships, establish traditions, and make memories.

A community-service focus, on the other hand, places more emphasis on rescuing others. So we decided to close our doors when it came to allowing friends to stay with us more than a day or two. We stopped offering to store items that didn't belong to us. We established "family hours" dedicated to spending time together as a family—away from outside visitors.

Choosing the nesting function for my home also made it easier to de-clutter. I decided what to keep based on functionality rather than on the notion that items might be helpful to somebody else someday. If it didn't enhance my home for the benefit of my family, I felt free to toss it.

## KEY 3: RUN WITH PASSION

Olympic runners know how delicious pizza tastes. It's good food, but it may not be the best choice for the serious and passionate athlete. Does the way you run your household reflect your passion to de-clutter? Do your decisions align with your desire to reach the finish line?

We're often forced to choose between what is good and what is best. When you make choices, align your decisions with your desire to de-clutter.

□ Want to buy the sweater you've been drooling over? The price may be good, but if you don't need it, it's best not to buy it.

□ Interested in scrapbooking? This hobby adds collections of special books, papers, cutters, and other numerous supplies. It's a good thing to organize your pictures. But is it the best decision to start a new, time-consuming activity involving buying, organizing, and storing more stuff? Probably not until you pare down what you already own to a reasonable level.

□ Thinking about taking a class on something that doesn't require supplies? Consider the time and energy it drains from your ability to de-clutter. Investigate the hidden costs in the activities you say yes to—such as drive time and prep time. When choosing between good and best, the best decisions align with your desire to de-clutter.

What should you say yes to?

□ Need proper organizing tools? Then go ahead and buy them. If you have a multitude of books lying around with no home, say yes to purchasing a new bookshelf.

□ Tired of those hard-to-clean blinds? Replace them with some new drapes.

□ Interested in a class on financial stewardship? Improving money management skills helps us make wiser decisions about spending money, which ultimately brings less clutter and bills into our homes.

## KEY 4: RECRUIT RUNNING PARTNERS, TRAINERS, AND CHEERLEADERS

Do you know anyone willing to run alongside you as you de-clutter? Invite others to join your team. Running partners, trainers, and cheerleaders make de-cluttering fun, stimulate motivation, and add accountability.

My friends Jan, Lynn, and Holly each possessed unique areas of expertise. Jan's motto is "Just throw it out!" She helped me de-junk while teaching me what to keep and what to let go.

Lynn enjoyed sorting papers. She handed me a life preserver during the times I felt I was drowning in an ocean of papers. Holly was my cheerleader; her support was priceless. When others criticized or questioned the items I threw away, she applauded my efforts. Her enthusiasm encouraged me to make bolder decisions when it came to ditching the clutter—like throwing out my six-foot, artificial Christmas tree.

Choose your trainers and cheerleaders with care. One of my friends gave me a million reasons to keep the junk I was getting rid of—this is not the makings of a good trainer.

Involve immediate family as part of your support team. They may not care to help you with the cleaning, but maybe they will agree to encourage you by acknowledging your efforts. Initially, my husband groaned at my plea to join the de-cluttering band-wagon. But when I asked him to encourage me, he cheerfully complied. Eventually, he caught the passion to de-clutter on his own, without any nagging from me. Turns out, de-cluttering is so much fun that it's contagious.

## KEY 5: REST AND REFUEL YOUR BODY

All that mental and physical energy spent on cleaning is exhausting. An overworked body requires a break, and a tired spirit needs rest. Take a day off now and then.

Take care of yourself and, if necessary, give yourself permission to take a break from the de-cluttering.

Once you complete your training, your new superior knowledge and skill will take you places you never dreamed of going. Like where you can invite friends inside your home without fearing they will run the other way. Or where you can wake up without a mess waiting to be cleaned. Or even somewhere you actually enjoy living.

### HOMEBUILDING

*Do you not know that in a race all the runners run, but only one gets the prize? Run in such a way as to get the prize. Everyone who competes in the games goes into strict training. They do it to get a crown that will not last; but we do it to get a crown that will last forever* (1 Cor. 9:24-25).

What is it that you are living—or running—for? What prize are you chasing? Clean homes and earthly gold medals don't last. Pursue the eternal treasures, the heavenly medals from a spiritually disciplined lifestyle. Become rich in relationships, not stuff.

What does your training regimen look like? Does it include disciplines such as prayer, worship, and confession? Funny how we spend paychecks on diet pills and hours at the gym to achieve a prize of physical beauty yet neglect giving our spiritual muscle a workout. We'll find time to read every organizing book and master each new technological gadget, but we are too busy to study the ultimate training manual—the Bible. Let's make the race for God a priority.

## De-Cluttering My Heart

Lord, forgive me for:

Lord, thank You for:

Lord, help me with:

## De-Cluttering My Home

How serious am I about getting my house in order? In what areas do I need the most training?

How do I desire my home to look, feel, and function? What am I willing to give up in order to achieve this?

Who would make good homemaking coaches? List individuals along with their areas of expertise. Invite them to join your team.

# 4 PUT YOUR HOUSE ON A DIET

**"THE** first step out of clutter and chaos into peace, joy, success, and order in your life is to become aware of how your organizationally impaired mind works. Being organized really is a matter of MIND management."[5]

Just as an overweight person cannot become thin in 24 hours, neither can the overweight house lose all of its clutter in a day. Maintaining weight loss and maintaining a presentable home both require a lifestyle change. A person who wants to lose and keep off the weight must replace or modify certain behaviors. Likewise, a person who wants to transform a messy, cluttered home must eliminate the attitudes and habits symptomatic of "stuffitis."

Years ago, crash diets leapt into the forefront of the news. Weight disappeared fast, only to come back with a vengeance. Slimmer for a short time, crash dieters gained more weight than they lost. Our homes face the same scenarios.

Growing up, our house got cleaned for events such as birthdays or holiday dinners. We feverishly cleaned the morning of the party, quickly preparing for company. I vacuumed before the guests arrived while my mother boxed up the clutter. I remember how she pushed and shoved to get those boxes into the coat closet. It didn't matter to us that our coats hung on the railings of the staircase instead of in the closet because the house was clean. Or at least it looked that way to us.

But after the guests left, the mess crept back, leaving us wondering why we couldn't keep a presentable-looking home. This crash cleaning for special occasions didn't work, and it made room in the house for more clutter. With every closet crammed with junk, more stuff piled up on the floor. Whether crash dieting or crash cleaning, both involve temporary change and don't lead to long-term success.

Attitude adjustment is necessary. When we change the way we think, our behaviors follow. Practicing new behaviors establishes new habits. Only then will we see permanent change.

So where do we get our attitudes and habits? Early in my decluttering journey, I realized my heritage as a descendant of a family stricken by the Great Depression impacted my battle with too much stuff. Leftover philosophies of the Depression, handed down from generation to generation, affected my way of thinking when it came to deciding what to keep. Back then, when belongings were scarce and money was scarcer, it made sense to hold on to things. And my family held on to everything.

My great-grandmother saved the lard from cooked bacon to use as a butter substitute. Fifty years later, she still lived like she did during those hard times, keeping the bacon fat to substitute for cooking oil. She embraced thriftiness. I recall the butter tubs she saved long after she could afford Tupperware. But she actually used those empty dairy containers. They weren't just sitting around in her cupboards for looks.

Today, if we were to save the bacon fat, it wouldn't be for recycling purposes. We'd hold on to the lard as a keepsake. If we collect plastic butter tubs, it would be to fulfill our new motto of "He who dies with the most containers wins!"

Survival was the mind-set of those who lived through the Great Depression. They ate everything on their plates because that might be all they'd have for a while. We either waste portions of our supersized meals or use our bodies like garbage disposals for the excess food we might feel guilty about tossing. It never occurs to us that we pile too much food on our plates. Or too much stuff in our dwellings.

In my family, Great Depression philosophies were passed

down, but the rationale behind them changed. We went from need to greed. My great-grandparents cherished spending time with friends and family and trusted in the Lord. In my immediate family we focused our attention on material possessions, becoming emotionally attached to our stuff. We began to trust in *things*. So we accumulated more stuff, bought bigger houses, worked more hours to pay for it, and struggled to keep clean homes.

Where did you get your attitude regarding possessions? Who taught you to keep all those items that steal space in your house and time away from loved ones? Where did you learn what to keep and what to throw away?

Stop assuming that everything you learned about keeping stuff is true. If your home is ever going to lose the weight, you need to educate yourself about the myths that tell you to hold on to the clutter. Let's explore these fallacies ingrained into us that encourage us to keep too much stuff. It's time to set the facts straight!

**Myth 1:** "I might need it someday."
**Fact:** By the time you need it, you won't know where to find it. What about all those things you need now that you can't find because all those things for "someday" are in the way? It's time to get rid of it.

**Myth 2:** "If I throw it away, I will need it in just a few days."
**Fact:** This is a poor attempt to disguise the "I might need it someday" excuse. A friend once shared with me this definition of junk: the things you throw out today that you discover you need two days later. Wrong. Junk is junk is junk.

I don't know of anyone who immediately found a use for something after getting rid of it, but I have seen friends exaggerate the definition of *immediately*. Funny how "two days later" suddenly equates to 12 months later. You hear people with this mentality say things like:

- □ "See! If I hadn't given away that extra coffeemaker last year, I wouldn't have to buy one now!" (Of course, you have to buy one only because the glass pot is missing amid all that clutter.)

☐ "Don't you wish you had saved all of Johnny's baby clothes now that you are pregnant again?" (You are nodding in agreement. Johnny is eight years old. You're expecting a girl.)

☐ "Honey, I told you not to sell your spare set of hand tools in the garage sale. Now, you will have to lend out your good titanium, Craftsman deluxe set." (The garage sale was more than six months ago. And who says you must lend out something just because you own it? Yes, it's good to share what you own, but be wise in determining what you're willing to lend and to whom.)

☐ "If only I had saved my bell-bottoms from the '70s, I wouldn't have to buy any now that they are back in style." (You were a skinny teen in the '70s. You are now a pleasantly plump grandma.)

☐ "I should've kept that second set of pots we got for our wedding. I could sure use them now!" (After celebrating your 20th wedding anniversary, you finally decide to replace the set you've been using these past couple decades.)

People overly attached to stuff can always find a reason they should have kept their dearly departed junk no matter how long ago they got rid of it.

**Myth 3:** "I might fit into this again someday." Let's not forget the more official sounding, "I am dieting right now so I can fit into it when I lose the weight."

**Fact:** So what if you fit into your old clothes again? If that happens, treat yourself to some more up-to-date fashions instead. Let's face it, most of our "skinny" clothes are at least a few years old. (Side note: The only valid reason to keep clothes that don't fit is if you are pregnant right now. If your baby is more than a year old, it's time to chuck your BP—before pregnancy—clothes and buy some new ones.)

**Myth 4:** "Ownership is always an asset."

**Fact:** From a different perspective, ownership is a liability. Everything we own demands time, attention, and money. Things cost money to insure, maintain, and clean. Possessions drain mental energy because we think, dream, and worry about our stuff. Our collections of things clutter not only our homes but also our schedules. We make time for our stuff—to use it, fix it, sort it, clean it, and organize it. We sacrifice relationships so we can spend more hours at work for extra income to buy things that can't love us back.

**Myth 5:** "It is good to have extra for backup."
**Fact:** If your toaster breaks, go buy a new one. You won't have to open a brand-new five-year-old toaster that was stored for back-up.

Yes, there are times to stock up. Nobody likes to find out the last person in the bathroom used the final square of toilet paper. But let's be reasonable. Plan out in a thoughtful manner what extra items to purchase based on how fast they are used.

**Myth 6:** "But I can't throw it out! It was a gift!"
**Fact:** You can throw it out, so do it! Ask yourself if you really love it. If the answer is no, toss it.

"But it would be rude!" I know; I once thought that way too. But a true gift is given with no strings attached.

Remember, the gift was a token of love. Throwing it out does not mean you are rejecting that person or his or her love for you.

**Myth 7:** "It might be worth something (now or someday)."
**Fact:** If you think it is worth something now, research the value. Check the Internet. Call an auctioneer. Go to the library. It's probably costing you more to keep it than what it might be worth.

If you think it might be worth something someday, consider the potential return on investment. Will it cost you more to keep over the years than what you would make from the appreciation value? Account for the hidden costs of storing it, cleaning it, maintaining it, and insuring it.

**Myth 8:** "All I need are some more storage bins."
**Fact:** Storage bins are not the cure but just a Band-Aid. They address the symptom (junk and clutter needing a home) but not the problem (too much stuff).

**Myth 9:** It's sinful or disrespectful to throw out religious trinkets, medals, pictures, symbols, and so forth.
**Fact:** Getting rid of religious clutter is permissible. Remember the verse that talks about seeking first the kingdom of God? Well, how can you seek first the kingdom of God while living in a kingdom of clutter?

When my mother passed away, a friend helped with the decluttering. Medals were taped to walls, doors, and windows all over the house. Our friend refused to throw this stuff in the garbage, fearing God's wrath would come upon her. That's superstition. God won't condemn you for eliminating clutter from your home. Medals and statues are inanimate objects. They're just things.

Do you recall the Bible verse that tells us to store treasures in heaven where thieves cannot steal and moths cannot destroy? Religious paraphernalia is not treasure in heaven.

Religious items in and of themselves do not bring us closer to God. Consider that grandparents who display countless pictures of their grandchildren will not automatically create a close relationship with them from the photo shrine. Time invested with them builds closeness. So it is with God.

You're not disrespecting God when you get rid of the broken crucifixes, cheap medals sent from fund-raising campaigns, or undisplayed statues. In essence, you show respect by making room for Him in your home and heart by removing clutter, even the religious kind.

**Myth 10:** I cannot keep a clean house because (insert excuse here).
**Fact:** When you want something badly enough, you will find a way to make it happen. I know the excuses because at one time or another, I used them.

☐ Too busy to clean? Then drop some activities.

☐ Children require your constant attention? Get a babysitter.

☐ Don't have enough storage space? Let go of some of your possessions.

☐ Job too mentally or physically draining? Cut back on hours or get a new career.

☐ Never learned how to clean? Find someone to teach you.

As my attitude changed about holding onto possessions, I stopped placing such tremendous value on clutter and noticed significant improvements that lasted more than a day. It hurt when I first pared down my clutter collection. But after a day's recovery, I was ready to let go of more. Like a good gym workout, I stretched my de-cluttering muscles and became even stronger the next day. My house lost so much weight that even I felt skinnier. Are you ready to put your house on a diet? Start today!

### HOMEBUILDING

*Do not conform any longer to the pattern of this world, but be transformed by the renewing of your mind. Then you will be able to test and approve what God's will is—his good, pleasing and perfect will* (Rom. 12:2).

Where does the renewing of the mind begin? It starts with asking God in prayer to change your heart.

Read the Bible. Study God's Word. Spend time with Him in a quiet corner of your home and pray. Be transformed by building a relationship with your Heavenly Father, through Christ His Son.

## De-Cluttering My Heart

Lord, forgive me for:

Lord, thank You for:

Lord, help me with:

## De-Cluttering My Home

Where did I get my ideas about what to keep and why to keep it?

What mental obstacles are keeping me from parting with things I really should let go? How can I overcome these obstacles?

In what ways do I place inflated value on my possessions? What might keeping all these possessions be costing me in terms of relationships, a clean home, and money?

# 5 PLAN YOUR ATTACK

**"WE** have more things per person than any other nation in history. Closets are full, storage space is used up, and cars can't fit into garages. Having first imprisoned us with debt, possessions then take over our houses and occupy our time. This begins to sound like an invasion. Everything I own, owns me. Why would I want more?"[6]

My baby's nursery hid somewhere amid the bags, boxes, and bins of stuff. With a delivery date just around the corner, I faced some serious cleaning in that room. Not long after, with a precious baby in my arms, cluttered rooms still tugged for my attention.

It seemed with every two steps forward, I took one step back. For each load of laundry I completed, another pile of clothes continued to grow, lurking in an overflowing hamper. When stacks of paper were tossed in the trash, it seemed like double that amount pummeled my mailbox. I was making progress, but not fast enough. With each victory, a new obstacle appeared in front of me. Every time I got the house clean, something happened—like a clothing sale at the mall or Christmas.

Sure, I recognized that I couldn't de-clutter in a day, but this was getting ridiculous! I needed a game plan.

Does my story sound familiar? Have you also made progress only to see it disappear? To pinpoint the obstacles hampering your progress, take a personal inventory.

Remember the definitions of clutter related to our very own behaviors? Which clutter-inducing behaviors do you fall prey to?

Which ones set the stage for new collections to invade your home?

## TAKE INVENTORY

*In what ways do you put the needs of others above your need to de-clutter?* Desiring to be a good friend, I seldom said no to the requests of others. If anyone wanted a place to store something, our home was open. If people needed a place to stay, we would bend over backward to make room for them.

*How do you express love and gratitude?* I showed love for friends and family by bestowing large numbers of gifts. Of course, I enjoyed buying and wrapping all the presents, and my husband relished the fact that he didn't have to do anything.

*What are your shopping habits?* Boy, was I addicted to shopping! A trip to the mall was like a treasure hunt as I searched for the best bargain on more junk to fill my home.

*How do you view books?* There's just something special about books, something captivating about owning my own little library. Now these bound pages of "sacred" reading—and I am not talking about the Bible here—were like pearls and rare gems that could not be tossed. Never mind that many of these treasures were stored haphazardly in boxes or flung on a bookshelf every which way.

*How many clothes do you own?* I complained I had nothing to wear even though my closets—and dressers, hampers, and floors —were filled with an abundance of shirts, sweaters, pants, jeans, blazers, skirts, and dresses. In fact, a number of outfits in my piles of dirty clothes were brand-new, tags and all, never worn. There they waited, wrinkled and undiscovered, as the styles grew obsolete and the seasons changed.

*Is your calendar constantly full?* Countless activities once erupted from my calendar. I had something scheduled for almost every day—except cleaning.

## GROUND RULES FOR BATTLE

The plan of attack begins with setting boundaries—defining

what is acceptable and what is unacceptable by setting limits. Think of boundaries as the ground rules for our battle with clutter. They are the lines we draw to guide us in what we will keep and what we will toss. They are tools for establishing behavioral standards in our homes to prevent clutter.

Here are some of the boundaries I set:

1. *My house is not a storage facility available for public use.* As much as I would like to help my friends with storing their stuff, I have too many things of my own to take care of. (Maybe that's why my friends don't have clutter problems—they just store their things in the homes of others.)

2. *My house is not an extended-stay motel.* Nor is it a dorm with openings for roommates. It is my family's sanctuary. If friends or family need a place to stay for an indefinite length of time, I decline their request to move in with us—even if it's only temporary. Even if they have a compelling reason. My family is my first responsibility. Therefore, I will not allow other people's emotional and physical clutter to reside in my home.

3. *I will not shop for fun, leisure, or to ease emotional pain.* If I don't see it, I'm not tempted to buy it. I will shop from lists whenever possible to avoid impulse buys—or should I say impulse clutter? I will also not use shopping as a means to medicate a hurting heart.

4. *I will establish physical boundaries for my possessions.* I will keep no more clothes than what fits in the closet. No more books than what fits on the bookshelf. I will not allow my home to become overrun with toys. My children will have age-appropriate boundaries on how much they are allowed to keep.

5. *I will evaluate scheduling new long-term commitments or taking up new hobbies without giving up a different activity.* The more activities I am involved in, the less energy I have to devote to my home. The more hobbies I undertake, the more collections of hobby-related items reign in my household. An overloaded schedule causes tiredness and burnout. Therefore, I will seek balance, carefully considering my goals and priorities. When choosing between good and best, I will go for best.

## THE GAME PLAN

The attack plan calls for more than just setting boundaries. We must now use these ground rules to establish an offense and a defense. When we are on the offensive, we sort, toss, and organize stuff we already own. The defensive approach involves taking specific actions to prevent clutter from entering our homes.

*The best offense is a good defense.* This rings true not just in sports but also with de-cluttering. Here is why: we're already overwhelmed with the amount of stuff in our homes. We finally see some progress, but our efforts become sabotaged by the influx of new papers, clothes, and toys that sneak in through our doorways. At least, that was my experience.

## DEFENSE

So, how can you play active defense? I'm glad you asked!

1. *Get your name off mailing lists.* Ever notice all the junk mail creeping into your home? It invaded my home with such vehemence that I swam in it. I got into the habit of setting it aside to open later, but later never came. Piles of junk mail overtook my kitchen counters, but I couldn't just toss it all away without checking it first. Occasionally, what looked like junk mail actually had something of value in it—like a refund or a check. So what can we do to prevent all these marketing letters in the first place? Simple. Contact the Direct Marketing Association (DMA).

Send a letter to the DMA requesting they remove your name from its mailing list. Be sure to include your name, home address, and signature. Give them all forms of your name, including nicknames and initials, to ensure you are completely removed. Here is the address:

Mail Preference Service
Direct Marketing Association
P.O. Box 643
Carmel, NY 10512

2. *Get your name on the "no call" list for your state.* Telemarketer interruptions steal precious time from your family and suck

energy from your day. At best, they are a nuisance. At worst, they convince us to buy whatever they're selling—something we didn't realize we needed until they called to sell it to us.

Start thinking of telemarketers as clutter sellers. Decide that you will not purchase anything from a telemarketer. Ever. And get your name off their list. Visit the following Web site to register for the national no-call list: https://www.donotcall.gov.

Consider making your number off limits as a contact number when friends transition to new homes. If there is one thing worse than a telemarketer calling you, it's a collector looking for your friend. I learned that the hard way. Protect your friendships by protecting the privacy of your phone number.

3. *Tell credit bureaus to stop selling your information.* Did you know that credit bureaus sell your information to bankers and insurers? That's where credit card companies collect data to market "debt" so you can buy more stuff. Sure, they say they are selling you credit, but in reality, they are selling you financial clutter in the form of debt. More monthly statements arrive via mail requiring payment for increasing amounts of things you probably didn't have the money to buy in the first place. To opt out, call 1-888-567-8688.

4. *Consolidate wherever possible.* Review your money habits. Can you close or consolidate any bank accounts? What about retirement accounts? Credit cards? Remember, the fewer the monthly statements, the less paperwork you have to file.

5. *Attrition activities.* Review your activities. List them. Which ones encourage purchasing more materials? What hobbies add to your paperwork? Can you drop any? Even if the paperwork and other related materials are minimal, reducing activities gives you extra time for yourself and more time to devote to home and family.

## OFFENSE

Let's move to offense. Here, the arena is our home. Our adversary is clutter. And we are at war!

No matter which room we clean first, successful de-cluttering tends to follow a pattern. Generally, a good rule to follow is On-ly Handle It Once (OHIO). However, severely cluttered rooms call for a more intense battle plan. When in the trenches, it is not always easy to let things go the first time we encounter them. Often, it takes multiple passes.

### The First Pass: Toss Trash

Find the garbage and toss it in the trash. Sell or donate things in decent condition that you know you don't want. If you have doubts about what to do with some items, set them aside to decide on later. If selling or donating unwanted items means they will be sticking around more than a week, don't hesitate to put them with the trash.

### The Second Pass: Group Friends

Ever hear that birds of a feather flock together? Well, find things that are "friends" and put them together. All photographs in one box. All paperwork in another. Continue to separate be-longings into categories. Christmas decorations, stationery, com-puter supplies, books, and so forth. Toss whatever you can, whenever you can. Don't get bogged down with evaluating every single thing. Keep the focus on putting like items together.

### The Third Pass and On: Sort and Organize

Once belongings are grouped together, they need to find a home or leave your home. This is the time to sort and organize the individual papers, trinkets, clothes, and other items.

## LET THE BATTLE BEGIN!

### Start with the Kitchen and the Bathroom

If no other rooms in your house are clean, at least get reason-ably clean the rooms where you clean yourself and cook your food.

### Next, Move to Your Bedroom

Why not the living room before your bedroom? Easy. We tend to take our bedrooms for granted. This is usually the first

## De-Cluttering My Home

What boundaries do I need to establish? How can I enforce them?

What is my defensive plan? What will I do this week to prevent additional clutter from entering my home?

What is my offensive plan? In what room will I start?

# 6 YOUR GRIME-FIGHTING ARSENAL

**"CLEANING** supplies should be stored in their own eye-level storage space whenever possible. It's so much simpler to retrieve cleaners and replace them after use from such a cabinet than from the dark and crowded dungeon under the kitchen sink."[7]

What kinds of things do you think would be helpful to de-clutter your home? Storage bins? Extra shelving? Closet organizers? Be careful. If not used correctly, these handy tools transform into clutter keepers.

I once thought if I could afford to buy more storage bins, I could keep a clean house. I'd have a place to put all the mess. If I had more shelves, my things wouldn't lie around because they'd have homes. If my closets were designed more efficiently, piles of junk wouldn't fester in them.

Then I learned the issue was with my desire for too much stuff, not my lack of storage. After months of complaining about not having enough room in the kitchen for all my kitchenware, my husband installed extra cabinets. He added eight cabinets and four drawers, three small shelves, and a long counter. This additional counter became a clutter magnet. I stored so much junk in those cabinets, I forgot what I put in them. I soon dis-covered more storage often means more stuff.

My problem was not my storage space. My problem was the excessive amount of food, dishes, party supplies, and miscella-neous kitchenware I wanted to keep. Organizing and storing clutter was not the answer. I needed to cut down on the amount of things I owned and stop purchasing more stuff.

So what is my point? Cool organizing gadgets and extra storage do not solve problems for the stuffaholic. But while we work on dousing the flame of our desire for excess, we still need some strong weapons to fight against clutter. Instead of storage bins, we need to think trash bags. It's time to stop storing the clutter and start eliminating it. Let's begin by building a home arsenal of tools to aid us in de-cluttering and cleaning.

## WEAPONS OF MASS DE-CLUTTERING

The defeat of the onslaught of clutter that attacks our homes calls for specific weapons. Use these weapons for picking up the mess, separating the meaningful items from the junk, and organizing valuables. Notice that storage bins are not among the weapons of mass de-cluttering.

**Trash bags** are the major assault weapon in the war against clutter. When you toss personal items for donation, use black trash bags. You might be tempted to keep something you see in a clear bag. If you can, spend the extra dollar on the heavy-duty kind when you're doing major de-cluttering. I like Glad Force Flex bags. There's nothing that makes you want to quit for the day like watching all the trash you've collected fall through the bottom of the trash bag.

**Wastebaskets** should be where your family will actually use them. If a certain area is a natural trash zone, then work with it by placing a wastebasket in the vicinity. Make throwing away trash convenient and accessible by placing receptacles in places near the hot spots where refuse accumulates. When we give our trash a home, we won't find it scattered about. Wastebaskets—they're not just for kitchens and bathrooms anymore.

**Boxes** are necessary for sorting extreme clutter. Use them to put "friends" together. When you know exactly how much you have, you make informed decisions on what to keep.

Don't waste time going to the grocery store for the freebie boxes. Visit an office supply shop and ask for bankers' boxes.

Moving boxes also work very well. Using boxes that are all the same size and shape encourages organization. Plus, they're easier to store during long-term de-cluttering jobs. Use them for trash or donations as you clear them out.

**A calendar and an address book** are wise investments. I use the Franklin Covey Day Planner, but any brand is fine. As you come across bills, write the due date in your calendar. Mark birthdays and appointments you want to remember and throw out the reminder notes written on scrap paper. It's time to toss all those old envelopes you're keeping for the return address labels. Put that information in your address book.

**Filing cabinets** provide a safe home for important documents currently scattered around in different drawers, closets, and other hiding places. The best kind is one with all-locking drawers. I learned that lesson when my baby discovered how to open drawers and threw a paper-flinging party.

When filing papers, use manila folders and put them inside the green hanging file folders. Don't forget to label your folders.

**Laundry supplies.** It's funny how clothes find their way into almost any room. Take an empty laundry basket to areas hit by clothing missiles. Think of your hamper as a wastebasket for clothing. Arm your laundry room with a sufficient amount of detergent and fabric softener so you can wash those clothes right away.

## WEAPONRY STORAGE

As soon as you clear a surface, clean it. You will probably find a layer of grime on those shelves, cabinets, and counters that have had junk perched on them for so long.

Dirty counters attract clutter. They tell us that no one cares what we place on them. Sparkling counters cry out to put items back where they belong. They beg us to preserve their good looks.

Let's get our cleaning supplies ready. What's that? Not sure where you put yours? Don't feel like finding them? I understand. Let me help solve this dilemma.

Where do you typically store your cleansers? Do you keep them in the dark recesses under the kitchen sink? That's what

I used to do. Canisters got pushed to the back. Spray bottles spilled. Trash bags ripped. Leaks dripped on stuff and created a gunk dust coating. I didn't care to bring out the cleaning supplies when the counters needed a good wipe-down because it was too hard to get to the cleanser. And I certainly didn't want to pull everything out just to find the one item stashed way in the back.

Maybe you store some things under the kitchen sink and other things in other areas. I confess that I did the same thing. Then I started taking lessons from the professionals to create a better system.

Have you ever noticed how businesses store their cleaning supplies? They keep a janitorial closet. Items are easy to find and easy to reach. If you don't have a closet, do you have a cabinet or maybe even an armoire you can convert into a cleaning and de-cluttering supply arsenal? Find somewhere that makes a convenient home for the basic necessities for housekeeping. It must be easily accessible so you can grab the supplies when you need them.

I cleared out two kitchen cabinets for cleaning items. What a difference! When I began storing my grime-fighting weapons in this convenient spot, I became more inclined to use them. Today, things get cleaned more quickly and more frequently. I know exactly where to find every item and it's not such a bother to get to them.

## GRIME FIGHTERS

With so many cleansers on the market, it's hard to keep track of which ones to use for which jobs. In the same way we accumulate an excessive amount of clothes, food, toys, and other material things, we accumulate a slew of cleaning supplies. We add to our clutter by purchasing different brands of various types of cleaning agents that perform the same function. Our grime-fighting weapons turn into the very thing that started this battle—clutter.

My friend Jan, the de-cluttering and cleaning expert, helped me compile a list of items I need for cleaning. You may notice some things missing. Jan's secret is simplifying. For instance, instead of buying furniture polish that builds up over time, she dusts her wood furniture with a wet paper towel. Review the list below and evaluate the grime fighters stocked in your arsenal. Determine how fast you go through them so you do not stockpile too much or get caught with too little.

□ *Rubber gloves:* There are some things you just can't clean without them.

□ *Sponges:* Throw used sponges out at the end of the day. They absorb more than water. They pick up germs and bacteria that quickly multiply in the moist environment sponges provide.

□ *Rags:* Washcloths, dish towels, and special cleaning rags fall into this category. Use what you like, but pull out a fresh one each day.

□ *Soap:* Dish soap is good for more than dishes. It cleans floors, countertops, glass, and just about anything. I buy the degreasing formula dish soap because it saves me from making room for a degreaser.

□ *Bleach cleanser:* These are also referred to as all-purpose cleaners with bleach. Clorox Cleanup is my favorite, perfect for killing food bacteria on the kitchen counter. Check if this is safe for cleaning your surfaces because it does contain bleach.

□ *All-purpose cleaner:* Fantastik and Formula 409 are examples, but remember that you only need one. All-purpose cleaners now come in all sorts of variations like oxy-fresh, orange-fresh, and kitchen-fresh. Just pick one—they all do the same job. Use all-purpose cleaners on surfaces unsafe for bleach.

□ *Window cleaner:* All you need is soap and water to clean windows, but spray cleaners like Windex are great for quick fixes.

□ *Squeegie:* These are what you use at the gas station to clean your windshield. They make them for home cleaning now too. Use them on shower doors and glass surfaces.

□ *Toothbrush:* A must-have for cleaning hard-to-reach crevices.

□ *Paper towels:* Whatever brand is on sale will work fine.

□ *Powder abrasive:* Comet is the perennial favorite in my circle of "cleanie" friends. Great for commodes, tubs, sinks, and more.

□ *Air disinfectant and deodorizer:* Lysol and Febreze are both excellent products. I like to use Lysol for "sick" germs but prefer Febreze for everything else.

□ *Baking soda:* I use it mainly for neutralizing strong odors.

□ *Bathroom cleanser:* These are the soap scum dissolvers that also remove tough lime and mineral deposits. The talk of the town agrees that LimeAway is the latest and greatest for this task.

□ You can also go online and find recipes for making all sorts of cleansers with vinegar and/or baking soda.

Think about keeping cleaning caddies in rooms like the kitchen and bathroom because these places demand constant attention. Fill a plastic caddy with your favorite supplies and store it in an inconspicuous place in those high-maintenance rooms. At a minimum, keep all-purpose cleanser, bleach cleanser, window cleaner, a toothbrush, and paper towels in this mini-arsenal.

## THE BIG GUNS

What about the bigger cleaning supplies like mops and brooms? I call these the "big guns" because of their size. For houses without janitorial supply closets, get creative on where you keep them. Don't store them in your entranceways. That's where my gram kept hers. A mop propped in the corner and the scent of cleaning supplies won't say "welcome" like a vanilla candle and a cleared entryway.

*Broom and dustpan:* Before you mop, sweep up the junk on the floor. Get a regular-size broom for large areas and a hand-sized broom for easy cleanup of smaller messes.

What kind of broom? One with nylon bristles. Straw brooms shed, causing faster wear and tear. Plus, who wants the extra work of sweeping up the shredded bristles?

*Paper shredder:* In this day and age, a paper shredder is a must for protection against identity theft. One little credit card offer in the wrong hands can cause big problems.

*Vacuum:* Yes, the vacuum is a great de-cluttering tool. It sucks up those dust bunnies and saves us from allergens attacking our home.

What kind of vacuum do you own? Is it heavy and cumbersome? Hard to use? Consider treating yourself to a new one. It's worth the money. I recommend you steer clear of the kind that needs to be assembled for each use or that requires you to fill a basin of water. These might be OK for a "superclean," but stick with a low-maintenance-style vacuum for everyday use. I learned this lesson firsthand. With my aversion to cleaning, a vacuum with parts to assemble only motivated me to find something else to do. I dreaded preparing the vacuum for use more than vacuuming itself. One that just plugs in and switches on is much more appealing for getting the job done, not to mention kinder to your pocketbook.

For small messes, get a cordless handheld vacuum. These work great for quick cleanup of spills. Keep it in a storage area close to the entryway for easy access during the months when mud is likely to get tracked inside.

If you own a multilevel home, consider purchasing a vacuum for each level. I don't know about you, but I get enough of a workout from cleaning without hauling a vacuum up and down the stairs. Think about getting a broom and mop for each floor as well.

*Swiffer:* If you haven't used these products for dry and wet-mop cleaning, you owe it to yourself to give it a try. They have revolutionized cleaning day at my house. It will cost a little more to use Swiffer than it will to use the traditional mops and brooms, but the results are fantastic.

## DANGER: PACK RAT CROSSING

A word of caution. Beware of the "yuckies" ready to besiege you when moving anything that hasn't been touched in a long time. Spiderwebs, dead bugs, and even critter feces may await you. What kind of critters? Let's put it this way. The term *pack rat* was not invented because it kind of rhymes or sounds cute. Clutter attracts rodents. Rats and mice make homes in places filled with lots of stuff. Clutter makes great nesting material. If you come across this, you will be thankful for arming yourself with the necessary cleaning weapons.

### HOMEBUILDING

*For though we live in the world, we do not wage war as the world does. The weapons we fight with are not the weapons of the world. On the contrary, they have divine power to demolish strongholds* (2 Cor. 10:3-4).

Another word for *stronghold* is *addiction*. All the storage bins and trash bags in the world cannot mask our addiction to stuff.

What is at the root of your addiction? Do you surround yourself with stuff because your heart stings from rejection, sexual or physical assault, emotional abuse, or something else? Does insecurity cause you to think you need things "just in case"? Were you fed a diet of too much stuff as a child, ignorant of the addictive qualities of material possessions? Or is it plain old greed?

Possession overload is often a heart problem. Seek God to heal your broken heart, then pray for wisdom and ask Him to help you do battle with past hurts.

## De-Cluttering My Heart

Lord, forgive me for:

Lord, thank You for:

Lord, help me with:

## De-Cluttering My Home

What de-cluttering and cleaning supplies do I need to buy to get my home in order? What weapons do I already own?

Where do I store my cleaning agents? Is there a better place to store them that is more easily accessible?

What can I learn by evaluating how professional businesses clean their buildings? What are some of the cleaning techniques used by restaurants, hotels, stores, and offices that I might adopt for better results in my own cleaning routine?

# 7 TAKE YOUR KITCHEN FROM CHAOS TO CLEAN

**"THE** kitchen is one of those spaces where we tend to accumulate huge volumes of items we never use. We collect vast quantities of mugs, dishes, souvenir glasses, food, pots and pans, serving platters, odd utensils, and plastic containers with missing lids, and rarely have enough storage space to keep them all."[8]

The battle plan is drawn. Our proficiency in de-cluttering causes even our family members to run for cover. Now it's time to attack the mess. Let's get dirty cleaning that kitchen.

## A TRIP IN TIME

Travel back in time for a moment to visit my messy kitchen. You'll see piles of dirty dishes, pots and pans heaped on the stove, a stuffed refrigerator with magnets and papers covering the door, mail scattered across countertops, groceries setting out in the open while the pantry overflows with food.

Take a good look around. What else do you see? Disorganized cabinets complement overstuffed junk drawers. The space between the ceiling and upper cabinets is topped with a hodgepodge of decorations and kitchen supplies. The linoleum floor is sticky, and there are debris pockets under the table.

Yikes! Where do we start?

Let's step back into the present, but now we're standing in your kitchen. Maybe yours is neater, or maybe it isn't. But regardless of the caliber of the mess, we'll begin at the same starting point.

# THE KITCHEN STRATEGY

## Begin with the Trash

Is your trash receptacle full? Then take out the trash and replace it with a new trash bag. Fill it with whatever trash you find. Look around for things like junk mail, empty cartons, ratty sponges, and old food. Shred anything with your name or personal information printed on it.

## Clear Flat Surfaces

What is stacked on your counters and tabletop? If mail, receipts, invoices, and other papers float in your kitchen, grab an office box and pile them all together. Set aside current bills to avoid late fees and disruption in services. If you have a functional paper-handling center, file items that need to be saved. If you don't have any type of paper organization system, do your best to sort through the box. Only keep what is necessary. You will learn what is OK to toss as you create a filing system that works for you.

Put away items that don't belong in the kitchen. Send runaway toys home to the toy chest. Jackets go back in the coat closet. Return books to the bookshelf.

Check your upper cabinet tops. Are they serving as storage shelves? Grease and moisture from cooking settle in this area, coating stuff with an oily film. Dispose of items not valued enough to keep in a clean place and find safe homes for the valuables.

## Attack the Dishes

Start with the piles of dishes in the kitchen sink. While you're there, determine which dishes you really need. Are there any you can live without? This is a great time to toss them.

How dirty are your dishes? Do you find plates with thick layers of mold-encrusted food sticking to them? If it's so disgusting that you don't want to clean it, would it matter if you pitched it? Here's a little secret—new dishes aren't that expensive. I've seen full sets at discount stores for as little as $20. If your dinnerware is ugly, scratched, spaghetti stained, or otherwise unattractive, go ahead and treat yourself to a new set. Just remember to throw the old set out.

How many sets of dishes and silverware do you own? When was the last time you used them all? Sure, keep extra for entertaining, but be reasonable. My cupboards used to overflow with dishes. It somehow seemed wrong to get rid of them, but once I pared them down to serve our family plus a few extras for guests, it made cleaning and organizing a lot easier.

After slimming down my dinnerware, I still had a beautiful set of stoneware collecting dust in the closet. My husband insisted on saving it. He wanted me to promise to use those dishes only on special occasions. I finally persuaded him to open the good set by pointing out that keeping the ugly ones sends a bad message. Refusing to use the nice stuff communicates a lack of respect for ourselves—that we are not worthy of anything other than second best. Furthermore, I reminded him that every day is a special occasion. Once each day is gone, we don't get it back again. Please, don't let your nice dishes languish in the back of a cabinet. Use them or lose them, even if it's just once a week for Sunday dinner.

Pots and pans—now there's an interesting topic. Growing up, my family owned so many pots and pans that they stored some in the basement. Learn your cooking style to find the number and types of cookware right for you. What ones don't you use? What would happen if you got rid of them? Do you own another pan that could do the same job?

And while we're on the subject, let's talk storage. I highly recommend a pot rack. It's so nice to have just what you need hanging right there where it's handy. Whatever you do, please, do not store your pots and pans in the oven. One of my many childhood cooking traumas occurred when I preheated an oven filled with pans. It cast a permanent shadow on my future as a baker. My husband will verify this.

I think it's a rule somewhere that every household must have every baking pan and utensil ever made. Guess what! I love breaking rules, at least the ones that invite clutter. How many cake pans, bread pans, muffin tins, potato mashers, egg whisks, cheese graters, and other fancy cooking supplies do you own? Be honest. When was the last time you used a potato masher? I didn't even know such a thing existed until I got one in a set of cooking utensils I received as a wedding gift. But once I owned it, I couldn't get rid of it. I might want to make mashed potatoes. I had no clue what the egg whisk thing was for. I mean, don't you use a fork to stir your eggs?

What else clutters kitchens? I heard somebody say storage containers. Funny how we buy them with matching lids, but then the lids seem to disappear. They're like socks without mates. What kinds of plastic storage containers lurk in your cupboards? How many do you use? I don't mean over the course of your entire lifetime. In any given week, which ones hold leftovers? You can pare that collection down. When I de-cluttered my kitchen, I found Pyrex dishes with matching tops. They sure beat the plastic containers. I cook with them and store leftovers in them. Multipurpose is a good thing. Plastic bags with zipper-like closures also store food just as well as the containers. The great thing about those bags is you can throw them out after you use them.

Ask yourself the following questions as you assess your kitchenware:

- ☐ Do I really need it?
- ☐ How often do I use it?
- ☐ Is it easy to clean?
- ☐ Do I own another tool that performs the same function?
- ☐ Is it broken, chipped, or peeling?

Evaluate the cost of holding onto each item. The more you keep, the more you have to clean.

## Clean the Refrigerator and Other Appliances

How many magnets cling to your refrigerator door? Can you even see the fridge under all that clutter? Something as simple as removing the magnets and papers affixed to the door by magnets gives the illusion of a cleaner, larger kitchen. Minimizing the amount of vertical clutter also makes it easier to clean. Next time you want to wipe down the door, you won't have tons of stuff to take down and put back.

When you open the refrigerator, are you afraid packages will come tumbling out? A little overstuffed, are we? My fridge used to be like that, but not anymore. I don't understand how I ever functioned in the kitchen not knowing what forgotten items were stowed away in the back corners of the freezer. I wonder how I survived grabbing one item from the bottom while worrying about everything on the top falling down. It amazes me how much money I wasted buying food that was never eaten and eventually spoiled.

Here's the deal on the refrigerator. Because I only go grocery shopping once a week, things don't build up. I use what I buy. Food seldom goes bad. At the end of the week, when things look a little sparse, it makes for easy cleaning of the refrigerator shelves. We may not see lots of food when we open the fridge or cabinets, but we don't go hungry. We waste less food and save more money. What a delightful surprise to see the positive impact this new buying habit made on our budget. Try it, maybe it will work for you too.

Today, I get comments like, "Don't you ever buy food?" and "I can't believe your fridge is so bare!" But I ignore these remarks. We always seem to have more than enough for my family. And it's so nice to reach into my freezer, effortlessly grab what I need, and close the door without causing an earthquake from tumbling food items.

What about other appliances? Anything you can let go of? If you have a toaster and a toaster oven, do you need both? If you can't remember when you last used the waffle iron, must you keep it? Whether it's dishes, food, or appliances, we can't keep everything and keep a clean kitchen.

As you de-clutter, clean. Take a good look at the stove. Is there a buildup of black, crusty, burned-on food on the burner plates? Give yourself a break and buy new ones. Remember, dirt is clutter too. Pull off the knobs on the stove and run them through the dishwasher every now and then.

With all the cleaning products available, what one is best for the stove? That depends on the amount of dirt and grease at home on your range. For reasonably clean appliances, use an all-purpose cleaner or bleach cleanser and paper towels. Degreasing dish soap and a green scrubbie work better for harder jobs.

Clean appliances such as the microwave, blender, Crock-Pot, bread maker, and any others screaming for attention.

## Thin Out the Pantry

I never claimed to be Betty Crocker. That's why I buy her cake mixes. I remember my mom's cupboard was full of Betty Crocker products. If ever confronted with a brownie shortage, there'd be plenty at our house. My parents always kept the food shelves stocked. Duplicates and triplicates of spices and condiments jammed our cupboards. We had enough canned goods to fill a small convenience store.

So how much stuff do you buy for your pantry? I followed the buying habits of my parents, purchasing whatever was on sale and stocking up on tons of extras. I even stocked up on items I didn't particularly like. Today, I buy only what I need for the week. I keep a few extra staples on hand, but not to excess. Like ketchup. I must have my Heinz ketchup, but I only keep 1 for backup rather than, say . . . 10.

As you de-clutter your food items, take everything out of your cabinets. Throw away everything that has passed its expiration date. Consider tossing anything close to its expiration date that you are unlikely to use before it expires. Is there anything you don't particularly like? Then why keep it? Toss everything that doesn't please your palate.

Be intentional about which cabinets you select for storing dishes, food, and cleaning supplies. Place dishes in the cabinets closest to the dishwasher. Canned goods and food items go near the stove. Arrange your kitchen in a way that makes sense to you.

One last tidbit on cupboards: what's in the cabinet below your kitchen sink? I challenge you to completely clear it out. Are there things you forgot about? Any cleaners with funny rings or odors? How about runaway garbage? One of the best decisions in helping me keep a clean kitchen was to stop storing stuff under the sink.

## Clean the Floor

Technically, this could fall under de-cluttering flat surfaces, but we still want to do the floors last. Rule of thumb says to start at the top and work your way to the bottom. Any crumbs that fell while wiping the table get cleaned up at the end. The same goes for small pieces of paper, food packaging, and dust from items that sat like statues time forgot.

Sweep up the big stuff. Your Swiffer will pick up the rest. For extremely dirty floors, I recommend getting down on your knees and washing it by hand. Clean sticky floors with a warm, wet washcloth and dish soap. Do the same when supercleaning around the baseboards.

Try to maintain the floor as best you can while de-cluttering. You may not finish the kitchen in one day, but a quick sweep when something drops or spills will make the floor job a lot easier when you're ready to give it a detailed cleaning.

## Give Your Entire Kitchen the Eye

Inspect your work. Did you miss anything? Evaluate your organizing. What works? What doesn't work? What do you want to change?

In my kitchen, we no longer pile plates in cabinets as high as the shelves will reach or place different size bowls on top of each other. It makes it easy to get what we need without the trouble of taking the whole stack out to get a particular size plate or bowl near the bottom. We also removed one of the refrigerator shelves. I found one less shelf made more room for storing food. With the extra space, I could store taller bottles upright and have easier access to the smaller items.

Plan on experimenting to see which organizing systems work best for you. Investigate what motivates you to stay on top of things. Learn the strategies and products that make cleaning easiest for you.

Rome wasn't built in a day. And neither was the mess in your kitchen. Anticipate that it may take more time than expected to create the desired look. All the clutter that built up over the years takes more than a weekend to sort and organize.

Give yourself a pat on the back. We want to see progress, not perfection. Would you look at all that progress? Wow, I'm so impressed!

### HOMEBUILDING

*As Jesus and his disciples were on their way, he came to a village where a woman named Martha opened her home to him. She had a sister called Mary, who sat at the Lord's feet listening to what he said. But Martha was distracted by all the preparations that had to be made. She came to him and asked, "Lord, don't you care that my sister has left me to do the work by myself? Tell her to help me!"*

*"Martha, Martha," the Lord answered, "you are worried and upset about many things, but only one thing is needed. Mary has chosen what is better, and it will not be taken away from her"* (Luke 10:38-42).

When all we see is mess, it's easy to focus on nothing else. But some things are more important than cleaning. When was the last time you took a break from the busyness of life to spend a moment with God?

Invest more time than just a few minutes for some "fast food" prayer here and there. Slow down. Give the Lord your full and undivided attention. Like Mary, take time to sit at the Lord's feet and listen.

### De-Cluttering My Heart

Lord, forgive me for:

Lord, thank You for:

Lord, help me with:

## De-Cluttering My Home

What does my kitchen look like today? What is the source of most of my kitchen clutter?

How much kitchenware do I own? How much do I actually use in a typical week? What am I willing to part with?

Do I overbuy when it comes to food? How can I change my shopping habits so that I don't waste money and add clutter from purchasing food I don't need?

# 8 YOU CAN'T STAY AFLOAT IN A SEA OF PAPER

**"THE** way to bring order to paper quickly and efficiently is to have a place for every kind, a convenient place, and put it in this place as soon as it comes into the house."[9]

Got paper problems? I know how you feel. Bank statements, bills, magazine subscriptions, newsletters, newspapers, sales circulars, coupons, and credit offers. But the list doesn't stop there. There are store receipts, check stubs, school papers, work papers, clothing tags, grocery bags, packaging, notepad sheets, copy paper, and greeting cards.

Ever feel like you're swimming in bills? Beyond overall organization of paperwork, clutterbugs wrestle with bill paying. It's not necessarily because we don't have the money. We just have trouble keeping track of when we made the last payment and which payments are due now. Sometimes we misplace our statements, checkbooks, or remittance envelopes. We might even forget to balance our checkbooks, telling ourselves that we'll send in the amount due after we determine if we have enough in our checking accounts to cover the payment. In the meantime, interest charges kick in and late fees accumulate. Will we ever find a way to organize our papers so that we don't drown in them?

Paper clutter is like a wave of water flooding a ship filled with holes. We are the captains of our ships—our homes—and we need to remove the "water" so we don't sink in a sea of paper. In a real ship, we'd plug the holes to keep additional water

from coming in, bail the excess water, and set up a system to effectively control water flow on the ship. It's similar with paper.

## PLUG THE HOLES

How does paper enter your home? These are the holes you
need to plug. Get your name off mailing lists. Cancel unwanted
magazine and newspaper subscriptions. Stop purchasing so many
take-out dinners and fast food.

## DRAIN THE EXCESS WATER

One of the biggest problems I faced when attempting to organize my papers was determining what to keep. I thought I'd
play it safe and keep everything. But *everything* is really a lot of
stuff. Imagine moving boxes upon boxes of papers every time
you change residences. That's exactly what I did.

So what do we need to keep? Let's start with the things to
keep permanently. These are called vital records, and they include:

- □ Birth and death certificates
- □ Adoption papers
- □ Marriage certificates
- □ Divorce and annulment decrees
- □ Vaccination records
- □ Wills

The toughest decisions for me were determining papers necessary to keep for tax purposes. Check with your tax advisor for a
complete list, but here is the general rule of thumb. Keep the
following tax-related items for seven years:

- □ Year-end bank statements
- □ Dividend payment records
- □ Investment sales records
- □ Charitable contributions
- □ Credit statements
- □ Income tax returns
- □ W-2s
- □ Pension plan and retirement account records

- ☐ Loan agreements, payment books, and statements of discharge
- ☐ Cancelled checks and receipts for tax deductible items
- ☐ Medical receipts

If you have additional questions on what to save, visit the IRS Web site at www.irs.gov or call the IRS help lines at 1-800-829-1040 for individual tax questions or 1-800-829-4933 for business tax questions. Ask for publication 552, titled *Record Keeping for Individuals*.

Papers that needlessly flounder in our homes many times relate to items we no longer own. Keep the following for as long as you own the item:

- ☐ Automobile records
- ☐ Insurance policies
- ☐ Investment purchase invoices
- ☐ Property bills of purchase

And last, there are those papers we keep for personal reasons:

- ☐ Magazines: Put away the notion of someday reading the stack of magazines going back eight years. Articles are recycled every year. There's always another cool craft project, another exciting new diet, and another awesome date night idea in the latest issues. Unless you have a work-related reason for holding on to back issues of magazines, keep only the last month's and current month's issues.
- ☐ Books: Don't we all love them? But must we keep fiction novels after we've already read them? Are you really going to read them again? Let me tell you about this amazing thing called a library. We don't have to clutter our homes with books when we can borrow them like we would a video. In fact, you can rent movies and CDs at most libraries too. Part with all your fiction (OK, most if not all). Keep only the nonfiction works you know you will reference in the future. Review your cookbooks and evaluate if you honestly use them all. Say good-bye to the books that take up so much space in your house and shout hello to a soon-to-be clean home.

□ Old school papers: Our parents saved all our schoolwork from kindergarten on up. Then we save everything from our college years. Limit school papers to those that have relevance in your life today. If you insist on keeping some as memorabilia, pick out the ones you like most and put them in a scrapbook. But don't keep everything. In fact, if you have no emotional connection to your alma maters, why not let go of the yearbooks while you're at it?

□ Bad photographs: Why is it we can't get ourselves to toss pictures with a loved one's head chopped off, red-eye problems in every retina, and major focus issues? It's time for these bad photos to meet the trash. Don't be shy about getting rid of unflattering photos and excess duplicates either.

□ Personal correspondence: Be selective on the letters and greeting cards you keep. Is the card from someone who is now or at one time was an important person in your life? Did the sender actually write a personal message in the card or just scribble a signature? Do the letters fill you with delight or make your soul weep? Would the next generation find them a burden or enjoy them as a part of their heritage?

Let's start "draining" those papers. Begin by tossing the trash. Thin out paper boxes by eliminating the no-brainers like old catalogs, sales circulars, newspapers, coupons, and junk mail. Be mindful of throwing away anything containing personal information, especially documents containing anyone's Social Security number. Use a shredder to maintain privacy and protect yourself from fraud.

After sifting out the trash from your potentially important papers, put friends (papers on the same topic) together to sort later. Keep anything questionable, but toss what you know is not necessary to keep. Depending on the amount of papers, separate by topic in boxes, folders, or with paper clips. You will determine the destiny of any questionable items in your next sort before filing the stacks of papers.

Whatever you do, do not blindly throw boxes of papers away. Check for hidden cash, uncashed payroll checks, savings bonds, and other forgotten treasures. Who knows? Irreplaceable photographs may have found their way into one of those boxes of papers. Know what you are throwing out before you get rid of things. And again, shred papers with personal information—or at least tear them into small pieces.

## SET UP A SYSTEM

Prepare your paper filing tools for use. You will need:
□ Four-drawer locking filing cabinet
□ Manila folders
□ Green hanging file folders
□ Pens for labeling

I will give the information to create a basic filing system. Once you're reasonably organized, you can experiment with color-coded folders, fancy labels, and other more elaborate organizing techniques.

When creating a filing system, define categories for filing your papers. Label the main categories and develop subheadings under them. I found it confusing and overwhelming when I read all the potential categories and subheadings as I studied paper management. To simplify this process for you, I will show you what I did to create a system that works for me.

1. Identify the main areas of paper clutter. We all will have Vital Documents and Financials, so plan on including these two categories as a given.

2. Create a section titled Monthly Bills. Although this technically fits under Financials, this receives its own category because of its fluid and active nature. File bills, marking the check number and payment date right on the invoice. Record the confirmation number if given one and file it.

3. Evaluate the activities that fill your calendar and analyze the paper flow associated with each activity. Being highly involved in church, I felt this was a large enough area to warrant its own category. As a writer, I have tons of work-

related documents in the house, so I created a separate category titled Writing.

4. Insert a Personal category for hobbies and special interests. I like coming up with fun and innovative party and gift ideas, so I keep a folder for this topic. Christmas is my favorite holiday, and I enjoy making holiday plans and exploring new traditions. Christmas easily merits its own folder.

5. Allocate enough room for family members to file their own papers. Consider getting a mini-filing cabinet for children to use so you don't have to worry about them getting into yours.

Use my example as a skeleton, modifying the categories to meet your lifestyle.

## Financial

Place a large label on the file folder to identify where the financial section begins, doing the same for each subsequent category. I keep separate folders for the following:

- □ Individual Tax Years (contains copy of tax forms, W2s, end of year statements, and receipts for deductions)
- □ Tax Prep (contains W2s and yearly statements as they are received, as well as receipts for itemized deductions)
- □ Investments and Retirement Accounts
- □ Credit Reports (includes any correspondence to fix errors)
- □ Real Estate (home purchase and repairs)
- □ Insurance Documents

## Vital Records

Keep original records in a safe deposit box or fireproof safe. File copies at home for easy access. Add folders for items that apply to you, such as adoption or divorce certificates and other legal records.

- □ Birth, Marriage, and Death Certificates
- □ Immunization Records
- □ Medical Records
- □ Veterinary Records
- □ Résumés

- □ Wills
- □ Genealogy (copies of vital documents from deceased relatives)

## Monthly Bills

I wrestled with filing bills under their own heading such as phone, utilities, cable, and so forth, or filing them according to the month. Ultimately, I decided to file each bill under its own heading, but I try to keep the most current bill in front. Save no more than one year's worth of statements, unless you need them for tax purposes. How do you know if you need them for income tax? Only if you are using them for itemized deductions like a cell phone plan purchased for a business. I added one special category to keep bills waiting to be paid:

- □ Unpaid Bills (What can we do to keep track of our bills without creating a detailed spread sheet? Keep a separate folder on unpaid bills. On a blank sheet of paper, list your monthly bills, amount due, and due date. After you pay the bill, record amount paid and the date payment was sent. Include the check number and confirmation number, if applicable. This convenient tool gives you a quick big picture view of what's due and what's paid.)

## Church

If you're not active in church, where do you spend your time? What activities generate paper flow? Here are my spiritual paper makers:

- □ Ministry
- □ Bible Studies (each study gets its own folder)

## Writing

Writing is akin to a work-related heading. Do you own a home business? Do you bring your work home? Instead of a writing category, create a title that reflects your work. Here is how I break down my writing category:

- □ Story Ideas
- □ Contracts

- ☐ Marketing and Publicity
- ☐ Conferences
- ☐ Writers Groups

## Personal

What are your hobbies? Consider having a file for travel, recipes, fitness, decorating, or other areas of interest. These are a few of mine:

- ☐ Party and Gift Ideas
- ☐ Christmas
- ☐ Community Calendar

## Family

I created this category so other family members could do their own filing. My husband files his own work papers and hobby-related papers. When my son is older, he will have a file for schoolwork and enrichment activities.

Once you identify your main categories and label your folders with subheadings, sort through your papers again as you file them. Set a goal of organizing at least one box of papers per day. Expect to take a couple weeks to several months building a working filing system. It all depends on how many papers you have and how fast new ones continue coming in.

Do your best to keep your head above water and don't give up!

## HOMEBUILDING

*Let love and faithfulness never leave you; bind them around your neck, write them on the tablet of your heart* (Prov. 3:3).

What do you write on the tablet of your heart? Does it contain a to-do list of good deeds to perform? Are there scoreboards for repaying kindness and hurt? Or does it hold reminders of God's love and faithfulness?

De-clutter the filing cabinets in your heart. Instead of creating lists of things to do, ask God to start doing things with you.

Toss away the relationship checklists and stop keeping score. Think about finding a verse in Scripture that speaks to your heart. Write it on the tablet of your heart by memorizing it so you can access it anytime.

## De-Cluttering My Heart

Lord, forgive me for:

Lord, thank You for:

Lord, help me with:

## De-Cluttering My Home

How many years worth of papers am I storing? What would be OK to get rid of?

Do I have questions about keeping certain papers for tax purposes? Who is a certified public accountant I can call for tax advice?

Do I have a filing system in place? If yes, how can I change it to make it more efficient? If no, how do I plan to start one?

# 9 BEHIND CLOSED DOORS:
## BATHROOMS AND BEDROOMS

**"A** clean home is a happy home and cleanliness begins in the bathroom."[10]

## THE BATHROOM

Forgive me if I sound sexist, but I firmly believe that toilet cleaning is a man's job. Come to think of it, that goes for the rest of the bathroom too. My husband vehemently disagrees, so we share the task of bathroom cleaning. Unfortunately, there will be times when you must perform this stinky chore entirely on your own. Like, if you're not married or you have a husband who leaves this job to you. Yes, maybe you can hire a cleaning lady, but not everyone has that kind of money.

So where do we start? With picking up the clutter, of course.

### Pick Up the Trash

What kind of debris sits on the floor, in the tub, and on the sink? Look for empty shampoo bottles, toilet paper rolls, clothes tags, old makeup, dull razors, and any other obvious signs of garbage.

### Send Displaced Items Home

Scan the area for items that don't belong in the bathroom. Check for dirty clothes and used towels. Can't see the floor because of dirty clothes pretending to be bathroom mats? Pick them up and put them in a basket. While you're at it, you might as well add the real bath mats. Take the basket to the laundry room and get a load started while you finish cleaning the bathroom.

If the tub area is a "hot zone" for dirty clothes, keep a hamper nearby. Think of the hamper as a home for dirty clothes until they get washed.

Notice any bath toys? Are children's playthings overrunning the floor? Find a safe home for them. The bathroom floor is not a sanitary place for toys. Some people sprinkle when they tinkle and you don't want little hands playing with that. Also, beware of backsplash. Flushing causes microbial fecal matter to swirl in the air. The bathroom floor is no place for toys or clothes.

## Clean the Sink

What items are making a mess on the bathroom counter and sink? Common culprits found in the basin area include whisker shavings, hardened toothpaste, and soap slivers. If soap rings are a problem, start using liquid soap. Soap in a dispenser tends to leave less mess than bar soap. If your loving husband leaves shavings, buy some wet wipes and ask him to wipe the sink area when he finishes primping. In fact, leave the wipes out for everyone in your household. Make wipes available for easy cleaning of toothpaste, soap scum, makeup dust, fallen hair, and anything else. When the cleaning supplies are accessible, the cleaning is more likely to get done.

What does the faucet area look like? Befuddled by the gunk around the sink fixtures, I despaired at ever getting my bathroom totally clean. Then I read somewhere to use a discarded tooth-brush for these areas.

## Clean the Bathtub

I hear that some people clean the tub while taking a shower. Lathering up while spraying tile-cleaner doesn't cut it for me. When it's my turn to clean the tub, I take the spray bottle and wipe it down. It helps to get other family members on board by asking them to rinse the tub and give it a quick wipe-down after they use it.

To minimize tub clutter, buy bathroom caddies for each family member. Let them use their own personal carriers for washcloths, razors, soap, shampoo, and other personal sundries. No more bathtubs cluttered with everybody's personal soaps and no more rings around these items for you to clean.

## Scour the Toilet

My husband is a plumber, so he loves toilets. He views them as sculpted pieces of porcelain art. That's why this job belongs to him. Someone once said there's no better way to say I love you than cleaning the potty. When he does this, he certainly is speaking my love language.

Anyway, if you are stuck cleaning the toilet, grab your choice of cleaner. Spray around, on top, and inside the bowl just to the water line. Clean it off with a paper towel. By the way, it might be a good idea to wear rubber gloves for this job. Next, pull out that handy-dandy toilet brush. If the bowl is really yucky, just pour in some straight bleach and let it set about 10 minutes. Brush the inside until it looks pretty, or at least as pretty as the inside of a toilet can look.

Make cleaning easier by not putting decorations on the flat area above the water tank. Items here not only collect dust but also fall victim to backsplash.

A word of warning from my husband: please avoid using toilet tank drop-ins because they slowly eat away at the rubber gaskets in the plumbing. When you least expect it, the gaskets will fail and the toilet will overflow. That is one mess you won't want to clean up!

## Mop the Floor

This is the area I despise the most. My Swiffer only works for part of the floor. The bathroom is such a small space with odd-shaped fixtures to clean behind, so we need to find another method. That would be the good, old-fashioned hands and knees method. Maintain the floor during the week with some bathroom tissue. Wet it slightly and pick up what you can with it.

### Give the Bathroom a Second Look

Is there anything you forgot? Give the bathroom a quick inspection and take care of any areas you missed. Make sure soap is available for washing hands. Hang a clean towel for drying hands. Straighten wall hangings that look crooked.

## THE BEDROOM

What do you use your bedroom for? Sure, it is the place we sleep, but it has become the multipurpose room for many homes. Not just for sleeping anymore, we use the bedroom as an exercise studio, a home office, a storage facility, and much more. Sometimes we even use it as a kitchen.

Let's think about assigning a function for the bedroom. How about using it just to sleep—or at least primarily for bed rest?

One thing that makes bedrooms in model homes so appealing is the design. We don't see bulky exercise equipment or unsightly filing cabinets. Stacks of bins and boxes don't fill closets or cover the floor.

Let's de-clutter the bedroom by transforming it from a multipurpose room into a spalike palace of rest and relaxation.

### Pick Up the Trash

What litter loiters in your bedroom? Remove any dirty dishes and take them immediately to the kitchen. Throw out empty soda bottles, clothing tags, old magazines, and other trash.

If this is an area where important papers are mixed in with other mail or paperwork, throw out the obvious trash. Box up papers you need to sort to go through later.

### Make the Bed

A neatly made bed is a great cleaning motivator. There's something about having a focal point of eye-catching clean. Select a matching comforter set for a cleaner look. When linens match, the room looks less cluttered.

Check the bed linens. How many blankets and top sheets do you use to make the bed? Do you really need them all? Think about replacing those layers with one warm comforter. When I stopped using a top sheet and blanket, the bed got made more often. It decreased my laundry loads and added more space in the closet for other things. Double bonus there! Minimizing bedding not only means less stuff to clean and care for but also decreases time spent making the bed.

Before making the bed, consider the last time the sheets tumbled around in soapy suds. If it's been more than a week, put them in the washer. Use hot water with bleach to kill bed bugs nestled in the fabric. While the linens get laundered, continue cleaning the bedroom.

## Attack the Piles of Clothing and Accessories

Overwhelmed by the clothes, shoes, belts, hats, bows, sashes, and costume jewelry? I know how you feel. What accessories clutter your bedroom? But then I discovered fewer clothes equated to less laundry. And fewer shoes mean less to trip over. Let go of outdated fashions. Toss the ones that don't flatter or fit. If something isn't comfortable to wear, don't keep it. Get rid of items with holes, stains, tears, missing buttons, or broken zippers.

Although makeup and perfume are not technically accessories, they tend to accessorize our dressers. Take a moment to de-clutter these and other personal grooming items. Test perfumes for their scent. Some dematerialize faster than others, leaving them with an alcohol-base aroma. Throw away lotions with odd colors or globs of hard material in them. A good rule of thumb for open makeup is to toss anything that's been open for a year or more; eye makeup has a shorter life span of three to six months due to bacteria growth. Don't be afraid to throw away unopened makeup that's been setting around for a while.

## Clear Flat Surfaces

Just like cluttered counters make a kitchen look messy, cluttered dressers give the appearance of disorder. Keep a minimal amount of decorative items on your dressers. Try to keep the dresser tops as clear as possible. It gives the room a more spacious feel, plus makes the dressers easier to keep clean.

## Organize the Closet and Dresser Drawers

Make homes for your clothing and accessories. Treat them with respect. Don't just throw them in a drawer or a closet.

Assign specific items to your dresser. I once stored all sorts of things in my dresser—makeup, lotions, books, stationery, important papers and junk mail, money, gift items, you name it. When I needed a place to put my clothes, junk stole its space. Remember the purpose of your dresser drawers—clothes only.

A friend gave me this great piece of advice: use only one dresser. Limit items to clothes that don't need to be folded like undergarments and socks. Using a standard dresser with four drawers, divide them in this way:

Drawer 1: Undergarments and socks

Drawer 2: Bed clothes

Drawer 3: Winter seasonal (heavy sweaters)

Drawer 4: Summer seasonal (shorts and swimwear)

Change this formula to meet your needs. If you have extra drawers, design it so that it's easy to keep things folded and looking neat. A T-shirt drawer tends to become disorderly and draws more effort to straighten, but folding messy jeans takes little time and energy.

Let's take a look at the closet. Try to keep the floor completely clear. It's too easy for junk—and valuables—to get pushed in the back to no-man's land. Unless you have a walk-in closet, it gets difficult to find matching shoes with bunches of other stuff on the floor.

It's a lot easier and takes less time to hang clothes rather than fold them. Look in your dresser and determine what needs to be moved to the closet. Here is a list of items to get you started:

- □ Pants
- □ Skirts
- □ Dresses
- □ Blouses
- □ T-shirts
- □ Tank tops
- □ Vests and blazers

Try organizing your closet by the color of the clothes. Put all black tops, pants, and skirts together. Work the continuum of darkest to lightest, ending with whites. Put rubber bands around pairs of shoes to avoid lost mates.

A word on hangers. Avoid buying hangers of different colors. And forget about trying to color-coordinate clothes according to the hanger color. It takes more time matching things up—time you don't want to spend on cleaning. Plus, a rainbow hanger effect gives the closet a more chaotic appearance. Keep it simple.

## Vacuum the Floor

Don't forget to clean under the bed. Evict dust bunnies and other debris squatting under the box spring.

I find that if I put one thing under the bed, other items magically appear there. Kind of like one dirty plate in the kitchen sink invites more dishes, junk under the bed accumulates the same way. Some of my neat friends get away with storing gift wrap or shoes under the bed. For people like me, this area becomes a breeding ground for too much stuff. Make a rule to keep the floor under the bed clear of clutter.

If it's been a while since you've vacuumed under the furniture, go ahead and do it. You never know what kind of clutter you might find.

## Give the Bedroom a Second Look

Step back and take a look at everything. Did you miss anything? Do your last-minute straightening and fluffing. Enjoy your new oasis of rest. Sweet dreams!

 ## HOMEBUILDING

*Come to me, all you who are weary and burdened, and I will give you rest* (Matt. 11:28).

Do you feel burdened by housework? Does the thought of cleaning make you tired? Are you pressured by your responsibilities and the expectations others have placed on you? Have you asked the Lord for help?

When your mind is weighed down by the turbulence of life, let your soul find rest in the Lord. Seek Him out and He will steer you through the winds and rain. Give up control to the One who can walk on water and calm the storm.

## De-Cluttering My Heart

Lord, forgive me for:

Lord, thank You for:

Lord, help me with:

## De-Cluttering My Home

What does my bedspread look like? Is it in good condition or is it just usable? Do I find the color and style attractive? Does it need to be replaced?

How does my shower curtain look? Do my towels and bath mats match the color scheme? Do they have a clean look, or do they appear worn? What do I need to change to make it feel like a relaxing spa?

Do I keep suitably-sized wastebaskets in my bedroom and bathroom so litter can be easily dealt with and doesn't end up where it doesn't belong?

# 10 ESCAPE FROM LAUNDRY MOUNTAIN

**"DO** you want to know why they continue to multiply? Perhaps the reason is that you have too many clothes because you have compensated for not doing laundry by buying more clothes to cover this problem. Then you struggle for two days to finish it all, but it never really gets put away because your drawers are too full to put anything away. So then you live out of a clothes basket or the piles on top of the dresser or dumped on your bed or in a chair. After a while you can't tell the dirty ones from the clean ones, so they all get tossed back into the dirty clothes pile."[11]

## FROM PLAYPENS TO MOUNTAIN RANGES

"I don't have anything to wear!"

"I hardly have any clothes!"

"I can never find an outfit I like!"

Sound familiar? Do you complain about your lack of clothing yet your overstuffed closets and dressers tell a different story?

When I was growing up, my mother always had a mountain of laundry to wash. She kept a playpen in the basement where she piled the dirty clothes. I don't think she ever saw the bottom of the playpen once she started using it as a laundry basket. Add to that several large trash pails of dirty linens. I'm not talking about a kitchen-sized pail that one keeps under the sink. I'm talking about enormous cans that you leave in front of the house on trash day.

Do you struggle with mountainous piles of laundry? I once had that struggle too. But I didn't use a playpen. My dirty clothes just got thrown on the floor.

Then one day it occurred to me that the fewer clothes I owned, the fewer clothes I would need to wash. Wow! What a concept!

After already de-cluttering much of my wardrobe, I prepared to cast out the villainous linens that created mountains of work.

## FILLERS (SOCKS AND UNDERGARMENTS)

Let's start with what I call *fillers*. These are the smaller items that lurk in the piles of clothes. These are also probably some of the easiest to part with since most of us don't develop emotional attachments to things like socks and underwear. When it came to fillers, socks were my downfall.

How many lonesome socks do you have lying around? If there was a mating service for the collection of single socks that lingered in my home, someone could have become rich.

Rather than dealing with the hassle of pairing up my socks, I would go buy new ones. Of course, I never threw the old ones away. It's not like when we gain weight, we gain a sock size. I had no reason to throw them out.

One day, I decided to just toss them all with the exception of a handful of pairs. My plan was to start fresh. I bought two new packs of the same style and color. Less work to mate them after they're washed, right?

A king-size trash bag full of nothing but socks testifies to the mental weight and physical mass of fillers. Socks of all different styles and colors overwhelmed me when I thought about all the laundry waiting for me to wash and partner.

Keeping it simple helped me prevent the extra work of sock care.

What can you do about your fillers? Consider tossing them if you have too many. Don't worry about finding mates. Just find a place for them in the trash. Hold on to only that which you need. And, please, don't try to find other uses for them. Sure, you can use an old sock for cleaning, but remember the goal is de-cluttering. We can't keep it all and keep a clean house!

Now, let's talk about underwear. Here is the deal with undergarments. Put in the trash the ones with holes, poor elasticity, tears, and stains. Don't worry about washing them first. If you wash them, you might be tempted to wear them. We don't want them to get mixed up with the good stuff.

Plus, we are too valuable to be wearing things that belong in the trash. Let's treat ourselves with dignity and respect. If an item of clothing is so worn that it projects a low self-worth, just throw it out.

## ILL-FITTING CLOTHES

"This makes me look fat!"

"Nothing fits!"

"I can't wear that—it emphasizes all the wrong places!"

Have you ever said or thought that about your clothes? Come on, there must be something you own that is flattering. That beautiful outfit is probably hiding somewhere in all those piles of laundry!

So if you own all these clothes that don't work, why do you insist on keeping them? I know, they might fit someday. Or you can use the ones that fit for painting, right?

It's time to assess priorities. How important is it to defeat the laundry monster and bring this mountain of dirty clothes down to a manageable size?

Start with the piles of clean clothes. Ask yourself, "Do I really love it?" as you evaluate each item. Set aside anything that doesn't fit or flatter. Be sure to put them in a box or bag that will not become mixed with the ones you want to keep. Immediately, take donation items to the drop-off centers before you think of an excuse to keep them.

## LAUNDRY PILES

Still have too many clothes? It's time to start putting

"friends" together. Let's start with T-shirts. It's easy to accumulate lots of these. Find all your T-shirts. Pull them out of your dressers, closets, clothes baskets, and other hiding places. Folding them neatly, find a large surface to rest them on. Assess exactly what you have. Did you think only about 15 or so were out of sight only to discover the number is closer to 50?

It's hard to determine what to get rid of when we don't realize exactly how much we have. Do this with other clothing items as well.

## WARDROBES

What is your "style"? Think about the image you wish to portray by the clothes you wear. If an item doesn't fit with your style, consider tossing it. In the movie *My Big Fat Greek Wedding*, Tula tells her love interest that when they first met she was "frump girl." Whatever style you choose, like Tula, put away frump girl.

What says "beautiful" to you? There are many styles of beautiful. What looks nice on you may look like a fashion blunder on me. Keep the clothes that make you feel good when you wear them. What ones do you feel most confident in? Which ones make you look most attractive?

Let me share a story on this. I love sweatpants because they are so comfortable; but they do not say beautiful. While channel surfing one day, I came across a talk show episode where the theme was "I married a hot mama, but now all she wears is sweats!" I wondered if I could have been one of the women on that show. That was enough motivation for change. I didn't need so many sweatpants, so I decided to keep a couple of pairs specifically for the gym and tossed the rest.

What types of clothes do you need? Think about your lifestyle. How often do you dress up? Does work require fine business wear, casual wear, or something in between? What outfits are best suited for your hobbies and interests? Be realistic by matching clothing styles to your lifestyle.

Which items are easiest to clean? Dry-clean only means more work. We may not actually be laundering these clothes ourselves, but we still have to drop them off and pick them up, not to mention the cost of having them cleaned. Keep items that require dry-cleaning to a minimum.

Which items are most versatile? These are the classics and tend to be solid colors so they can be worn with a variety of items. They are not faddish or trendy, but stay in style. They can dress down a business outfit or dress up a pair of jeans.

## LINENS

If all we had to wash were clothes, laundry day would be much simpler. But we still have towels, tablecloths, curtains, bedding, and other linens. If they are not bogging us down in the laundry room, they are still stealing valuable storage space.

How many towels do you need for each person living in your household anyway? I suggest starting with a maximum of seven, one for each day of the week. If you can do with less, then go for it. When I started de-cluttering, I kept about four for each member of my family. That seemed to work out pretty well. Keeping fewer towels may mean you have to wash them more often, but at least you won't have a mountain of them always waiting to be washed.

Do you use tablecloths? How many do you really need to keep? I discovered it was much easier to clean my table with a sponge after each meal than to constantly wash tablecloths. Figure out what works best for you.

How many sets of bed sheets is enough? My vote is two for each bed. This way, when you wash your bedding, you can make your bed with a clean set right away. It's a good idea to keep a few extra blankets for cold winter nights, overnight guests, or snuggling under while watching your favorite TV show.

## CLOTHING AND LINEN GUIDELINES

When determining which clothing and other linens to keep, ask the following questions:
- □ Is it ripped or torn?
- □ Is it frayed or faded?

□ Are there missing buttons or broken zippers?
□ Is it permanently stained?
□ Does it fit?
□ Does it flatter?
□ Does it match with anything?
□ Does it need to be dry-cleaned?
□ Do I have enough similar items that perform the same job?
□ Do I really need it?
□ Do I really love it?

## WASHING INSTRUCTIONS

Part of de-cluttering and organizing the laundry includes actually doing the wash. For years, I washed all my clothes in cold water because I didn't know what was safe to wash in higher temperatures. I never learned how to use bleach in the laundry, so I settled for dingy whites. But after de-cluttering my clothes to the point where only the good ones were left, I wanted to know the right way to do laundry so I could take care of my clothes. After interviewing friends with laundry expertise, I learned there is no one right way to do laundry. There are, however, some general guidelines.

Let's start with supplies. Every laundry room needs the following:

□ Laundry detergent: liquid or powder, it doesn't matter
□ Color booster: these are the "oxy" products that add an extra cleaning element to colors
□ Bleach: use 1/2 cup when washing whites
□ Bleach pen: this works great on whites that can't be bleached because of colored emblems or stripes
□ Trigger spray stain remover: use a color-safe spray-on bleach to remove stains on colors not safe for regular bleach
□ Fabric softener or fabric sheets: these are both optional, but I prefer dryer sheets when using a softening agent

Before washing, always do the following:

□ Check pockets for things like money and lipstick. I shudder to think of the clothes I ruined because of lipstick left in a pocket.

□ Close zippers, snaps, and hooks. This protects other garments in the same wash load.

□ Tie drawstrings. Trust me, pushing a string back out a centimeter at a time because the string got lost in the seams is no fun.

□ Remove unwashable belts, pins, and other accessories attached to garments.

□ Pretreat stains. Follow the instructions on the products you use.

□ Mend clothes with tears, broken zippers, missing buttons. Agitation from the washer can turn a small mending job into a major one.

□ Check all care labels on garments for special washing or drying instructions.

## What Is Permanent Press Anyway?

Most washers and dryers have a permanent press setting. When interviewing moms about their laundry routines, I was surprised to hear so many answers along the lines of "I don't know what that's for." Use the permanent press setting for clothing that tends to wrinkle. In the washer, this setting offers a cool-down period before the final rinse to prevent wrinkles. In the dryer, the difference is the heat setting—it's not quite as hot as the heavy setting. Again, this prevents wrinkles from forming in the dryer.

Use higher heat settings for denims, towels, and garments that don't easily wrinkle. Set the dryer to fluff air for delicates— or better yet, air-dry them.

## Prep Work

Everyone sorts laundry a little differently, but it all breaks down to whites, lights, and darks. For easier sorting, keep three baskets in your laundry room, one for each color sort.

The rule of thumb for washing is the lighter the color, the hotter the water. Check all care labels on garments for special washing or drying instructions. Hot water may be too harsh for a delicate white. Delicate knits sometimes need to be air-dried.

Start the first load doing whites that require bleach. Then move to whites and off-whites without bleach. Continue with colors from lightest to darkest. This helps prevent bleach particles that may have escaped the final rinse from ruining colors. Remember—never overload your washer.

## Whites

Whites include undergarments, socks, towels, and linens. Use a hot water wash. First, add bleach. Let it mix a little with the water, and then add soap. After the water finishes filling the washer and the agitator starts, add the clothes.

## Lights

For whites and off-whites such as blouses, skirts, and pants, use a warm water wash. Don't add bleach.

## Darks

Use cold water wash for colors. Do not add bleach. Turn clothing inside out to prevent bleeding and fading. Wash new clothes separately or with like colors and fabrics.

Moving on to the dryer. Check the lint trap before you start your load in case the last person to use the dryer forgot to clean it. Fill the dryer, but don't overstuff it. Toss in a fabric softener sheet and turn the dryer on.

Fold and hang clothes immediately when dry.

Now, let's de-clutter those dressers and closets and finally catch up on the laundry!

## HOMEBUILDING

*And why do you worry about clothes? See how the lilies of the field grow. They do not labor or spin. Yet I tell you that not even Solomon in all his splendor was dressed like one of these. If that is how God clothes the grass of the field, which is here today and tomorrow is thrown into the fire, will he not much more clothe you, O you of little faith?* (Matt. 6:28-30).

I constantly found excuses for keeping clothes that should've been tossed. They might fit someday. They may come back in fashion. They cost good money. What are some of your excuses? Yet, God tells us not to worry about our wardrobes. He will clothe us in more splendor than we can imagine if we follow Him. It's time we stop worrying so much about our clothes and start trusting in God.

## De-Cluttering My Heart

Lord, forgive me for:

Lord, thank You for:

Lord, help me with:

## De-Cluttering My Home

Why do I have so much laundry? What kinds of clothes do I have too many of?

What obstacles prevent me from de-cluttering my closets? What am I going to do about them?

How am I going to evaluate which clothes I should keep? What kinds of boundaries will I establish to prevent new clothing purchases from overloading my house?

# 11 THE DE-CLUTTERING SPREE

**"THE** first step of the . . . organizing process is . . . 'reducing the volume' or a 'gross sort.' What does that mean exactly? It means making the simple and easy decisions first and eliminating as much as you can—as fast as you can. It will give you an immediate lift, a great feeling of accomplishment, and help you see clearly what is left to deal with."[12]

Clutter inevitably spreads into any available open space. Like the manifest destiny of the Old West, these final frontiers of somewhat presentable areas give way to the expansion of too much stuff. It's time to reclaim our rooms by going on a home de-cluttering spree.

## ROOM BY ROOM

Living rooms, dining rooms, dens, home offices, rec rooms. Even attics and basements, not to mention garages. They cry for our attention too. Start with rooms used most often. Here is the general plan:

### Toss the Trash

Do a quick clean sweep with a trash bag and throw out obvious trash. Set aside items to donate to charity. Get donation items out of the house as quickly as possible.

### Clear Flat Surfaces

Start with the visible mess on tabletops, shelves, and floors. Last, move to the invisible clutter nesting inside drawers and storage bins. Send lost items home. Put homeless friends together, keeping similar things in boxes marked *sort*.

## Clean Furniture and Accessories

Wash removable couch fabric and couch covers. Clean bureaus, coffee tables, and desks. Dust lamps, figurines, and other decor.

## Sweep or Vacuum the Floor

If it's been awhile, move furniture for a thorough cleaning. Get underneath and behind furniture. Consider hiring a professional carpet cleaner to give your carpets new life.

## Check Your Work

Take a look at the room and fix anything you missed.

Here is a review of what to do for extreme de-cluttering:

*The first pass—toss trash.* Throw out obvious trash. Set aside belongings for donation and drop them off at your local charity ASAP.

*The second pass—group friends.* Place things in boxes according to category. Put friends together—Christmas decor in one pile, clothes in another, papers in another, and so forth.

*The third pass and on—sort and organize.* Sort through items in each box and find homes for them or toss them.

After you've de-cluttered the mess, consider what you can do to make visually displeasing rooms less of an eyesore and easier to clean. In my childhood home, the laundry machines were kept in an unfinished basement. It felt dark and murky down there. Cobwebs hung from the wood and pipes. I certainly didn't enjoy going down there. A finished look in areas like the basement or attic adds to the overall appeal of a home.

# GARAGE

Originally made for cars, garages today house everything under the sun. Lacking room for automobiles, our expensive cars sit in the driveway while our garages store assorted odds and ends of far lesser value.

It's time to clear out the garage and give it back to our cars.

☐ Get rid of the obvious trash.

☐ Group like items together to give you a big picture of how many of the same materials you own. As you sort through storage, ask yourself, "Do I really need it?"

☐ Set up an organizing system that gives homes to groups of items according to zones. Store friends together; gardening equipment against one wall, tools in another corner, automotive supplies on their own special shelf, and so forth.

Here are some ideas to make your garage more user-friendly:

☐ Make a Peg-Board for tools. Draw an outline in black marker to help you remember where each tool belongs.

☐ Create a workbench with cupboards and cabinets for construction supplies, but keep only those you need.

☐ Nail hooks in the wall to hang shovels and rakes.

☐ Seal cement garage floors. Sealant prevents clutter of the dust variety.

☐ Add drywall and a coat of paint for a finished look.

No matter how disorganized your garage looks, set a goal that it will always be clean enough to perform the function it was designed for—to protect your automobiles from outside elements. As you have time, organize the garage and add those special touches to make it comfortable for you and your car.

## DE-CLUTTERING THE SMALL SPACES

Once we tackle the visible clutter, we can focus on the invisible collections hiding in drawers, cabinets, and totes.

What do the insides of your drawers and cabinets look like? How many are organized? Which ones overflow with clutter? Analyze what does and doesn't work in each of them and learn from it. There's a reason most people use silverware trays. They effectively organize eating utensils.

And what about junk drawers—why create a place that gives a home to clutter? These temporary shelters easily become permanent residences. One junk drawer can multiply into several. I tried setting up "his" and "hers" junk drawers for my husband

and me, but when they filled up, there was nowhere else to stow the clutter. Rather than putting objects back in their assigned homes or making a decision on keeping items, we tossed everything in junk drawers. New ones popped up everywhere, even in places that were previously organized. Like chicken pox, the junk spread to every available drawer and cabinet in my home.

And what flounders on the bottom of your totes? Whether it's a gym bag, book bag, fanny pack, or purse, it attracts clutter. Common stowaways include runaway lipstick, forgotten packs of gum, scattered change, old receipts, lost checks, expired coupons, and the kitchen sink. Trash like hair from brushes, food crumbs, and candy wrappers reside at the bottom like sticky refuse in a garbage can.

Drawers, cabinets, and totes are black holes where stuff disappears, never to see daylight again. To thoroughly clean them, we need to completely empty them. Use the following technique for de-cluttering all types of compartments:

## Empty the Contents

Dump the entire contents from the compartment onto a clean surface, clear of clutter. Double-check corners and crevices. When de-cluttering purses, be sure to double-check all zipper compartments. For cabinets with multiple shelves, clear every shelf if possible. For larger cabinets, you may need to do one shelf at a time.

## Toss the Trash

Get rid of the garbage. Take note of the types of trash your tote, drawer, or cabinet collects. Let's examine refuse that tends to lurk in purses and learn how to prevent its accumulation:

- ☐ Sales flyers: When salespeople hand out brochures, do you accept them? Or does the marketing piece end up lining your purse? Learn to politely say, "No, thank you," or immediately toss the handout in the nearest trash receptacle.
- ☐ Candy: What snacks do you carry in your purse? Think about limiting the types of quick pick-me-ups you store in your handbag to breath mints and gum. No candy means

no melted chocolate, sugar pellets, or wrappers cluttering your purse. Plus, your waistline will thank you.

□ Receipts: Is your purse a dumping ground for every sales receipt and invoice you receive? Keep important receipts, invoices, and other related documents in a designated envelope. Toss the ones you don't need. File the items in this envelope on a weekly basis.

### Send Lost Items Home

What do you have in your drawers, cabinets, and totes that belongs somewhere else? Put those items away.

Remember the organizing rule of storing friends together. Assign like items to a specific place. Use organizing tools like mesh trays and labels to help drawers and cabinets remain orderly.

For purses and totes, store makeup in one compartment. Keep your wallet, cash, and checks in another. If you don't have enough compartments for what you like to carry, use minibags for storing like items.

### Clean the Drawer, Cabinet, or Tote Itself

Wash your purse according to the material. Use a damp paper towel or sponge to clean drawers and shelves. Add soap or other cleaning agent for stubborn dirt.

### Designate Totes, Drawers, and Cabinets for Specific Uses

As you decide what to store in these places that once housed clutter, consider the items that naturally gravitate into them. Do certain spaces tend to accumulate mostly office-type clutter? Then that might be a good place for office supplies. If the prescriptions in your medicine cabinet keep ending up in your kitchen cabinet, then clear a kitchen shelf for vitamins, medications, and other related items. Think about what you find in the clutter hot spots and work with the natural tendencies of where you place things.

## DESIGN IT CLEAN

Keeping a clean house is not just about de-cluttering and organizing. To a certain extent, how you design and decorate each room adds or subtracts to the intensity of housework. This is one lesson I wish I had learned sooner.

After de-cluttering my kitchen, I decided to buy a new table. The one I bought had beautiful carvings around the edge. Let me tell you, it was a pain to clean. When repainting my house, I selected a flat paint because it was cheaper. It rubbed right off every time I tried to clean the saliva our St. Bernard splashed all over the walls. And the list goes on. Learn from my mistakes. When remodeling and redecorating your home, remember to consider the following:

□ Bowl-style lighting catches bugs and moths. Cleaning out the dead insects adds to your chore list.

□ Chandeliers are nice to look at, but not so wonderful to clean. Taking down each crystal and individually polishing it requires a lot of time.

□ Furniture with lots of tiny crevices holds dirt tighter than a plain surface, requiring more elbow grease.

□ Furniture in different colors and styles gives the appearance of a cluttered home.

□ Big furniture or too much furniture makes a room look cluttered.

□ Sofa sets with patterns make an already cluttered room appear messier.

□ Flat paint is not as easy to clean as satin paint. Flat paint rubs off when scrubbing off dirt and wall marks *unless* a special type of sponge is used.

□ Electric stoves with flat surfaces are easier to clean than stoves with burner plates.

□ Fancy doorknobs on kitchen cabinets require more work than a plain doorknob.

□ Kitchen cabinets that go all the way to the ceiling prevent the tops from being used as shelves—which eventually collect a thick layer of grease from cooking.

□ Tiles on counters, floors, and tubs mean extra work cleaning the grout.

□ Faucets with knobs for hot and cold require more cleaning than a lever-style faucet. Placing faucets one inch away from the wall offers just enough space to facilitate cleaning those hard-to-reach areas between the faucet and the wall.

◻ A shower curtain is easier to wash than all the crevices in a track for shower doors.

◻ Blinds and jalousie doors (the kind with all the slats in them) are a pain to clean. Replace them with something simpler.

◻ Bulky curtains are more difficult to take down and more expensive to get cleaned. Curtains that require hooks for hanging are time-consuming to rehang. The loop style provides a quicker and easier setup.

◻ Unfinished rooms feel cluttered. Drywall garages, attics, basements, and other unfinished areas in the house.

◻ Cement dust is just another thing to sweep. Seal cement floors to prevent extra work.

## INEXPENSIVE TOUCHES

Remodeling and redecorating usually means spending a lot of money. When you don't have thousands of dollars in the budget to redo your home into a low-maintenance, easy-to-clean oasis, you can still add some inexpensive touches. As you de-clutter, allocate a little money each month for the little things, while tucking a few dollars away for the bigger things. Here are a few small touches you can add to your home without taking out a second mortgage:

1. Paint a fresh coat of color on living room walls.
2. Purchase quality doormats. Untold amounts of dirt and debris enter the home on the soles of shoes. It will lengthen the life of your carpet, save money on vacuum bags, and make less work. Place one on each side of entryway doors, including the garage.
3. Recaulk areas in the kitchen and bathroom where the caulking is discolored or loose.
4. Buy a new bathroom curtain to coordinate with your existing colors. If the budget allows, select a designer style to

replace the plastic curtain. In the overall scheme of things, a pricier curtain is still inexpensive. Don't forget to purchase some matching towels too.

5. Read Don Aslett's *Let Your House Do the Housework* (Betterway Books; rev. ed., 1995) for a comprehensive review of how to design a home with easy-to-clean fixtures and materials.

Wow! That's a lot of de-cluttering and cleaning. But the more we do it, the easier it becomes and the more fun we have. Keep it up!

### HOMEBUILDING

*I know what it is to be in need, and I know what it is to have plenty. I have learned the secret of being content in any and every situation, whether well fed or hungry, whether living in plenty or in want. I can do everything through him who gives me strength* (Phil. 4:12-13).

Contentment. This is the secret weapon in battling the world of marketing that tells us more is never enough. In times of abundance, be thankful. In times of need, trust in the Lord. But always embrace an attitude of contentment.

And remember to call upon the One who strengthens our souls. When we feel overwhelmed and doubt our ability to achieve presentable homes, call on God. Stand firm in the confidence that we can do all things and endure all things through Christ.

### De-Cluttering My Heart

Lord, forgive me for:




Lord, thank You for:

Lord, help me with:

## De-Cluttering My Home

What is the messiest room in my home? How do I plan to tackle that mess?

Where are some of the clutter hot spots in my home? What items am I inclined to leave out where they don't belong? How can I organize my stuff so that it's accessible to take out and easy to put away?

What steps will I take to intentionally design and decorate my rooms in ways that minimize cleaning?

# 12 OUTSIDE CLUTTER

**"CLUTTER** is like weeds—it keeps cropping up. But regular 'weeding' keeps it under control."[13]

Creating a beautiful home takes more than de-cluttering the inside of our houses. Let's not forget about the extensions of our homes—our cars and our lawns.

## AUTOMOBILES

Some people live in their cars. Or from the mess inside, you'd think so. My car has always been a clutter magnet. With a trunk full of storage and a mess on the floorboards, I struggled with keeping this small area clean, let alone my entire house.

In a way, our cars are extensions of our homes. We use them like the kitchen, chowing down our fast-food dinners. Turning them into mobile powder rooms, we brush our hair and put on makeup, sometimes while driving in traffic. Newer models have DVD players, just like our living rooms. Sometimes, our cars even act as bedrooms on long trips when we stop at a rest area for a quick nap.

Are you ready to transform your vehicle into a clean ma-chine? Then let's get started! Put a car care kit together to make it easier to clean and maintain these mini homes-on-wheels. Store your kit in an accessible area in the garage or in the trunk of your car. Please note that cars require special cleaning products because of the paint, waxes, finishes, and window tints. Here is what you need:

☐ Upholstery cleaner: Seats and floors get dirty. Use a special car-cleaning agent to remove tough grime. I use Stoner Upholstery and Carpet Cleaner. Many of these cleaners also work on the inside of your home too.

☐ Interior cleaner: The dashboard, steering wheel, console, and other interior surfaces require cleaning. Whatever brand you use, verify that it's safe for all areas. I like Meguiar's Quik Interior Detailer because it works on all the interior surfaces of your car.

☐ Extra-strength dirt remover: Keep a special cleaner on hand for hard-to-remove dirt like tree sap, tar, and sticky bugs. I prefer Meguiar's Gold Class Bug & Tar Remover because it's a trigger spray. Other comparable cleaners tend to be in aerosol form and contain scary warnings about extreme flammability.

☐ Glass cleaner: Not every glass cleaner is safe for car windows. Find one you like in the automotive department. My friends rave about Stoner Invisible Glass. It gets an A+ in my book too.

☐ Car wash soap: Regular dish soap can be harmful to automobile paint and finishes. Meguiar's NXT Generation Car Wash works well, but any brand is fine.

☐ Automotive wash mitt: It's kind of like an oven mitt, except it's used for cleaning cars.

☐ Cotton terry cloth or microfiber towel: Use these for drying your car. No using rags and old, shoddy towels!

## Start with the Trash

Throw out garbage on the seats and floors. Check for debris under the seats too. Don't forget the middle console, door pockets, glove compartment, and trunk.

## Send Lost Items Home

Remove everything that doesn't belong in the car and send it to its proper place. Start with the visible clutter on the floor and seats. Then move to under the seats, in between crevices, and inside compartments.

Designate storage areas in your automobile for specific items. Begin with the glove compartment. Start by completely emptying it. Limit items that go back in the glove compartment to essential paperwork and maybe a couple of pens. Keep registration and insurance together. Use a bright-colored envelope so you can easily find them if the glove compartment starts getting a little cluttered. Losing the registration and insurance in a sea of papers is not good in case you get pulled over by a police officer. File car maintenance records in an envelope in the glove compartment so they are readily available if needed.

Side pockets on doors serve as clutter bunkers. Just because you have a pocket to put stuff in does not mean you have to put anything in there.

I have yet to discover a functional use for the middle console other than storing garbage, clutter, and change. I call my console the clutter pit. To transform the console from a stuff keeper to a clutter fighter, place a brown paper bag inside to collect small trash such as receipts and candy wrappers. Designate it as a mini garbage pail to prevent junk and papers from littering the seats and floors.

Use ashtrays to hold spare change. These automotive piggy banks offer quick access to dollars and coins when approaching tolls or grabbing a quick drink at the convenience store.

What clutter fills the trunk? Check for things like clothes, food, books, toys, and trash. The trunk is not a second closet for our oversized wardrobe nor is it an extra pantry for our huge stockpile of nonperishables. It's not a bookcase, toy chest, or garbage pail either. Make a habit of maintaining a clear trunk with the exception of a few necessary items. Decide what is OK for the trunk, such as a first-aid kit, an extra blanket, a flashlight, a tire gauge, jumper cables, and windshield wiper fluid. And while you're in the trunk, make sure the spare tire has air in it and is in usable shape.

## Clean the Inside of the Car

Having no idea how to clean a car, I called on the experts with professional experience in detailing automobiles. They set

me straight about the right way to clean cars. I learned that
cleaning interiors is as easy as "ABC."

A. Vacuum interior, including seats, cup holders, ashtrays,
   and car mats. (I never would have thought of vacuuming
   ashtrays and cup holders!) Remove the car mats and vacuum the floor. For stubborn spills, dirt, and stains, use an
   automotive upholstery and carpet cleaning product.

B. Clean and protect inside surfaces, including vinyl, leath-
   er, and plastic with an interior detailing cleaner. Simply
   spray on a dusting cloth and wipe.

C. Clean the windows using an ammonia-free window
   cleaner. This will prevent damaging any of the window
   tinting that may be on your car.

## Clean the Outside of the Car

Sure, I've done fund-raisers where a bunch of us hosed down
a car with some sudsy water. But I never actually cleaned the
outside—or inside—of a car on my own. Deciding that I needed
to learn how, I again consulted the experts. Turns out, there is
an ABC method for the car exterior too:

A. Clean the outside of the car using automotive car wash
   soap. With a high-quality wash mitt, get the car good and
   sudsy. Start from the top and move down to the bottom.
   Rinse thoroughly.
   ☐ Do not use dish soap, as it is harsh on paint and strips
      wax protection.
   ☐ Use a dedicated wash mitt or wheel brush to clean
      your wheels. You do not want to contaminate your reg-
      ular wash mitt because it may possibly scratch the
      paint the next time you wash your car.

B. Towel-dry using a good-quality cotton terrycloth or
   microfiber drying towel.

C. Go over the outside of the windows with ammonia-free
   window cleaner.

## Give the Car a Second Look—Inside and Out

Did you miss anything? Make last-minute touch-ups and call

it good. But, if you really want to impress the neighbors (or your spouse), you can wax the car and shine the wheels. Sound like a lot of work? Surprisingly, it's not! Again, find a brand you like, but I tend to stick with Meguiar's Quik Wax and Meguiar's Hot Shine.

**Easy waxing:** I always pictured waxing a car to be a major task. In my mind, I compared it to polishing fingernails—something that needed to be carefully done with extra time set aside for drying. Except that a car is hundreds of times larger than a fingernail, so I figured waxing a car would be an all-day chore. Who knew you could wax a car in less than 30 minutes with a spray wax that you wipe like window cleaner? Want to try waxing your car? Apply a coat of wax protection using a spray-on and wipe-off aerosol wax. This type of spray wax not only makes the car look much better but also helps protect the paint from the elements.

**Shining tires:** I nearly collapsed the first time I heard about tire cleaning products. Want to know how to clean tires? Spray on the protectant cleaner and walk away. That's it—easier than using hairspray! We need more cleaning agents like this! These spray-on-and-walk-away products leave tires looking shiny and new.

Who knew cleaning a car could be so much fun? And even more enjoyable is driving a clean car!

## OUTSIDE DE-CLUTTERING

The outside of our homes reflect on us and contributes to the overall look and feel of our homes.

How do you think of your front lawn, driveway, and entrance to your home? Realtors refer to it as curb appeal. My husband calls it prime storage area for anything that won't fit in the garage. I compare it to the wrapping paper covering a special gift—a beautiful outside makes the inside seem even more beautiful.

Let's assess the outside of our homes. Consider these questions:

- □ How does your yard look? Is your garden nothing but a bed of weeds? Is the grass brown and fading? Could your lawn be mistaken for a field of tall grass?
- □ Is the paint on your house chipped or fading? Does moss grow on your shingles? Is your siding in disrepair?
- □ Do you keep several trash cans in plain sight? Does trash litter your driveway?
- □ Is your wood fencing and trim warping or coming apart? Are your metal railings and fences covered with rust?
- □ Is your front porch hidden by a jungle of foliage? Or is it a gathering place for dead plants?

Here are three simple steps for de-cluttering your lawn the quick way:

**1. Pick up debris.** Take lawn litter directly to the trash can.

**2. Send displaced items home.** Bikes go back in the garage, indoor toys back in the house, and so forth.

**3. Mow the yard.** Even if you don't rake the mowings, it'll still look better than a field of high grass.

Since we probably have enough trouble keeping the inside of our homes looking nice, we don't want to add extra work to clean and maintain the outside. What can you do to make your outside easier to manage? We gave up gardening. Though it's not like we ever really started it in the first place.

My husband and I love roses. We planted three rosebushes that bloomed cascades of beautiful flowers. That was with the first buds. One thing you should realize about rosebushes is that they require constant attention. We didn't know this. And so without proper pruning, these magnificent beauties turned into overgrown, weed-ridden clutter.

Think "simplify" and give up that which causes extra work or adds clutter.

## HOMEBUILDING

*The farmer sows the word. Some people are like seed along the path, where the word is sown. As soon as they hear it, Satan comes and takes away the word that was sown in them. Others, like seed sown on rocky places, hear the word and at once receive it with joy. But since they have no root, they last only a short time. When trouble or persecution comes because of the word, they quickly fall away. Still others, like seed sown among thorns, hear the word; but the worries of this life, the deceitfulness of wealth and the desires for other things come in and choke the word, making it unfruitful. Others, like seed sown on good soil, hear the word, accept it, and pro-duce a crop—thirty, sixty or even a hundred times what was sown* (Mark 4:14-20).

Are we the seed sown among the thorny weeds? Weeds—or clutter—choke the Lord out of our lives. Weeds need constant pulling so they don't kill the blossom. If we are to bloom, we need to make de-cluttering a habit. We don't want to hover in the shadow of thorns and thistles, missing out on the sunlight through a relationship with our Lord. We desire the water from the Holy Spirit to not be absorbed by the weeds, but to quench our parched souls.

It's time to do some gardening. Pull the weeds in your life—get rid of the thorns of worry, sin, and the desire for too much stuff.

### De-Cluttering My Heart

Lord, forgive me for:



Lord, thank You for:



Lord, help me with:

## De-Cluttering My Home

Do I use my car as a mobile storage container? What boundaries do I need to establish to prevent my car from looking cluttered?

Does the outside of my home look appealing? What can I do to make it more attractive?

What projects or hobbies am I willing to give up to free me from unnecessary work?

# 13 SNEAKY SABOTEURS IN YOUR CLEAN HOME

**"THINGS** are always wearing out, running down, getting old, falling apart, and dying. Scientists call this principle the Second Law of Thermodynamics, which means that everything is tending toward entropy. Simply stated, entropy means the tendency to disorder. Homemakers should have no problem understanding this principle! Things don't naturally get neater; they naturally become more of a mess."[14]

Do you ever start cleaning house only to be sidetracked by something else? This happens to me all the time. In fact, it's happening to me as I write this book. I'm thinking, "Look at this mess! And I'm writing a book about keeping a clean house?"

As the mom of a toddler, there are days I feel as if I am competing with my growing baby and he is winning. My boy likes to find stacks of books, papers, and pens to fling in the air while locating special hiding places for the remote control, phone, and car keys. He enjoys moving furniture to reach the kitchen faucet to dump pools of water on the floor. Then, when I try to get some rest, my little monkey jumps on top of me like a rodeo cowboy yelling, "Giddyup!"

When facing obstacles that hinder our efforts to clean, what can we do? Identify the saboteurs!

First, understand that our children are blessings, not saboteurs. They do what kids do—make messes. It's part of our job as parents to train them in the discipline of cleaning.

Saboteurs are the obstacles that work against us in performing our duties as home managers. These are the distractions that render us ineffective in all of our roles—not just the ones relating to keeping a clean house. Sometimes we call them excuses.

My biggest saboteur is busyness. I'm not really competing with my toddler in a battle for energy. I feel so tired because I give in to the rest of the world tugging on my schedule—time that's needed for mothering and homemaking.

Let's look at some of the saboteurs that prevent us from keeping presentable homes:

## TIME WASTERS

Playing on the computer, yakking on the phone, and opening junk mail are prime examples of time wasters. How many times have you opened computer solitaire for one game only to find yourself still playing hours later? I admit, I'm guilty. How often do you talk on the phone when you know you should be doing something else? I can't begin to count how many times I call my sister because I don't feel like cleaning. Sometimes junk mail disguises itself as an official-looking letter. Don't we all end up opening something like that at some point?

Other time wasters include watching TV, excessive napping, leisure shopping, and watching the wind blow by. Anything so we don't have to clean.

## BUSYNESS

My calendar was inundated with activities. I always had things to do, places to go, and friends to meet. People wondered about me, "Is she having an affair with her Daytimer?"

I didn't leave enough open time to focus on cleaning. On those occasions when I had the time, I used the extra precious hours to recuperate from my busy schedule.

I finally decided to set aside a block of time when I don't make commitments. This is called margin. Maintain free space in your calendar so the busyness of life won't trip you up in your housekeeping efforts.

## POOR HEALTH

Sometimes our homes suffer because of specific physical or mental ailments. Even something that seems as innocuous as the common cold can throw a wrench in our cleaning abilities. For individuals with chronic ailments, the best thing to do is see your doctors regularly and follow their advice.

When taking medicines with extreme side effects, others may have to help with the workload. If finances allow, hire someone to help you instead of expecting yourself to do it all with a broken leg. The housework will always be there, so take care of yourself first.

Clinical depression or obsessive-compulsive disorder (OCD) can interfere with the desire for a clean home. When I'm feeling down from a these-pants-make-me-look-fat day or a bad hair day, I'm not motivated to clean. I can't imagine what it must be like for someone who struggles with depression. If you think you suffer from depression or OCD, see a doctor immediately. Find a counselor willing to collaborate with a professional organizer. Accept whatever help you need to get your house and life back into order.

## EXHAUSTION

When we're too tired to clean, what can we do? If only it were as simple as taking an extra nap. But it's not that easy.

A pediatrician friend told me that when a baby has a fever, the fever is only a symptom of an illness. But we still treat the fever. Likewise, while exhaustion is just a symptom, we need to determine the cause to treat the fatigue. Busyness, stress, and poor health all contribute to feeling tired.

So how do we treat exhaustion? Allocate time for extra bed rest. Treat yourself to a massage. Drop some activities from your schedule. Slow down. Participate in a retreat. Eat healthier. Drink more water. Visit your doctor.

There was a time I experienced extreme fatigue. It was a major battle to get out of bed and brush my teeth. Physically unable to do much, the house was a disaster. I checked with my doctor so he could cure what I thought to be chronic fatigue syndrome. It turns out that total and utter exhaustion is a symptom of pregnancy.

## BARGAIN HUNTING

My husband says there are two seasons: church season and flea market season. During flea market season, he's faster than a speeding bullet getting in and out of our house of worship so he can hunt for bargains. Like a hunter circling his prey, he persuades the vendors into practically giving things away. (And he actually has been known to bring home dead animals—at least the taxidermied heads of them.) He impressed me beyond measure with his ability to find good things at cheap prices. After we stuffed our garage with all these amazing deals, we started realizing that maybe we don't need to buy something just because the price is right. Our eagerness to buy lots of inexpensive stuff sabotaged our goal of having space in the garage to park our cars.

Who can resist a good sale? If you lack that kind of discipline, avoid garage sales, flea markets, and auctions. Remember, one person's trash is not always another person's treasure.

## FREEBIES

Free stuff is fun. But it's not always good, especially when we're trying to de-clutter.

My sister accumulated an overload of toys and clothes for her girls because people gave their old stuff to her. She accepted anything people offered. When her friends got rid of stuff, they always knew they could dump it off at her house. It's OK to accept donations, but only if they're needed. It's so tempting to take something just because it's free.

Fairgrounds and festivals are notorious for their junk giveaways. Freebie novelty items abound. They give new meaning to the term *clean sweep* for clutterbugs. My mother loved going to the county fair because of all the freebies she could bring home. Her version of a clean sweep was not cleaning the house but clearing the freebie tables at the fair of all their goodies. If a booth was giving away pencils, she and her beach-bag-sized purse breezed along the side of the table as she casually swept them into her bag. Do you do that? Not in the same league as my mother, I never performed a clean sweep like that. But I am guilty of taking a few extra now and then.

## BAD HELPER BOUNDARIES

Most of us like to help others when we can. But sometimes we have to help ourselves before taking on the Good Samaritan role. Airplane safety procedures require passengers holding a baby to put the oxygen masks on themselves first. After the parent or guardian is getting oxygen, then he or she can take care of the little one.

How does this relate to de-cluttering? It goes back to not storing other people's stuff. But it also goes beyond that into the realm of saving clutter we think will help other people.

While visiting my sister a few years back, I noticed two large trash bags full of toys slumped on her kitchen floor. She explained the toys were for a friend. When confronted on how long these bags sat waiting to be picked up, she acknowledged them sitting there for "just a couple of months." Just a couple of months? That's more than eight weeks with junk cluttering her kitchen! Fortunately, her big sister (me) was there to set her straight.

When saving items to give away, tell the intended recipient it must be picked up by a certain date. If that bag of stuff is still there after the deadline, donate it or throw it out.

## ATTITUDES OF PROCRASTINATION

*For now* and *later* should be banned from our vocabularies. They are bad words, yet I humbly confess that sometimes I still use them.

"I'll just put that item here *for now*."

"Oh, I'll clean that up *later*."

Create permanent homes for things. Then you don't have to find temporary dwellings. A for-now attitude means more work later. Things stashed in places they don't belong add clutter to those areas. When we forget where we put things *for now*, we spend extra time later looking for lost items or purchasing duplicates.

Get into the habit of cleaning as you go. When you complete an activity, think "Clean *now!*" instead of "I'll get to it *later.*" Put away your belongings as soon as you're through with them and wipe up the mess. To avoid more work later, throw trash out immediately.

Just as compounding interest on a credit card leads to out-of-control debt, compounding interest on trash leads to out-of-control housework. Consider:

- □ We eat dinner. Food falls on the floor. We step on the food. Our footsteps create a path of crumbs. We set an important paper on the floor. It becomes encrusted with grease and crumbs.

- □ Newspapers are left all over the floor. They rip when people walk on them. The cat tries to eat the paper and tears it to shreds. The baby plays with the shredded paper and drags it all over the house.

- □ Mail gets tossed on the kitchen table. To clear the table for dinner, we stick it in the nearest drawer. We keep repeating this habit. The drawer becomes full. Then we have to sort through an entire drawer mixed with personal correspondence, bills, and junk mail.

## GIFTS

Gifts are probably the biggest saboteurs by sheer physical volume. Presents of all kinds crowded my house and cluttered my life. My obese home suffered from a lot of gift fat on both the giving and receiving ends. Gift clutter sprawled in every room. My family, friends, and I were generous to a fault—overgenerous.

You don't need to be everyone's personal Santa. It's OK not to give a sack full of presents to everyone you know for birthdays and holidays. Sometimes less is more. I've learned that when I give less, people appreciate what I give more.

For my husband's birthday one year I bought him a wheelbarrow and as many gifts as I could fit in it. He sped from one present to the next, ferociously tearing off the wrapping paper and barely pausing to see what I got for him. Now, I try to be creative and not overwhelm him with so much stuff. It makes the experience more special. He never lets me forget the Christmas I bought him a few small stocking stuffers and a wallet. Inside that wallet, I gave him $500 to buy what he wanted instead of a bunch of junk to clutter our home.

On the receiving end, I now find more joy in receiving fewer gifts. What's important is that I'm remembered, even if it's a phone call or a greeting card. For my birthday, I tell my husband that the best gift he can give me is cooking and cleaning for the day so I don't have to do anything. We may eat pizza on paper plates for breakfast, lunch, and dinner, but I'm happy because I get a time-out from my kitchen duties. (Note to Daddy: I still like getting cash in your cards!)

Simplifying our giving is key to defeating the saboteur that presents itself in beautiful wrapping paper and big, shiny bows. Let others know before holidays that you'd like to forego a gift exchange—or at least minimize it. Cap the number of gifts or limit the amount of money for each person to spend.

Before deciding on a gift to buy, don't just ask, "Would (name of person) like it?" Ask yourself if this gift will enhance that person's life or just add clutter.

Search for creative gift ideas. I started giving my nieces panties for birthdays and Christmas. Plain underwear doesn't make an impression, so I go the extra mile and pay a few dollars more for something I know they will like—such as panties with their favorite cartoon characters etched on them. I figured this makes a good gift because it's not clutter. Growing kids need new underwear.

What kinds of gifts make great presents and prevent clutter? Whether giving or receiving, consider the following ideas:

□ Family picture, framed
□ Time together, perhaps a treat to dinner
□ Babysitting
□ Entertainment tickets to a movie or play

- Entertainment book (a special coupon book sold across the country, usually associated with fund-raising)
- Food club membership
- Gas card
- Gift certificate to a restaurant, coffeehouse, or grocery store
- Gift card to a favorite department store
- Baked goods
- Certificate to a massage parlor or hair salon
- Cash

Become familiar with the saboteurs of your clean home before they cause problems. Then head them off!

## HOMEBUILDING

*Above all else, guard your heart, for it is the wellspring of life* (Prov. 4:23).

We guard our homes from thieves and people with ill intentions. Are we doing the same for our hearts? What saboteurs does your heart fall victim to—money, power, possessions, entertainment, work, unhealthy relationships? Don't give your heart to something that can't love you back—or to someone who won't love you back. Seek out safe relationships where you can be yourself. Start by offering your heart to God. Let Him be the source of your wellspring.

### De-Cluttering My Heart

Lord, forgive me for:

Lord, thank You for:

Lord, help me with:

## De-Cluttering My Home

What are the biggest saboteurs—or excuses—that prevent me from creating the kind of home I desire?

What changes can I make to defeat the obstacles that sabotage a clean home?

How do I feel about the way my family exchanges gifts? What suggestions can I make to maintain the valued traditions of celebrations while reducing the potential clutter?

# 14 MONEY TALKS, CLUTTER WALKS

**"WE** don't need more credit or more stuff. What we need is the courage to think for ourselves, the maturity to tailor our lifestyles to fit within our incomes, and the willingness to find contentment where we are and with what we have."[15]

One of the biggest excuses I've seen for accumulating clutter is saving money. We buy something because it's a bargain, not because we actually need it. We reason that we might be able to use it someday. And if we can't use it, we can give it as a gift, right? You just can't beat those sale prices. We think bargains save us money, but we fail to realize that every penny spent is one less penny saved.

Whether it's an expensive ornament, a cheap trinket, or a sale item, it's worth nothing if we don't need it, and it adds clutter to our lives. It's not a good deal if we won't use it. When we purchase too much stuff, the resulting clutter costs more than the few dollars saved.

"But what if I can't get the same thing later at this current low price?" you protest.

I have news for you. There will always be another sale.

I'm not saying don't buy sale items. My point is, don't buy something just because it's on sale when you don't really need it. Ask yourself these questions when you shop:

- □ Do I really need it?
- □ Do I really love it?

□ Can I afford it?
□ How expensive is it to maintain?
□ Is it easy to clean?
□ Regardless of cost, is this a quality item?
□ How often will I use it?

## SEVEN MONEY-SAVING TIPS TO REDUCE CLUTTER

### Pay Off Credit Cards

How many credit cards are nestled inside your wallet? Tired of the hassle of so much extra paperwork, I got rid of my credit cards. While most people like to keep one in case of an emergency, I made the move to shred them all. I can already hear those "But what if" statements coming.

□ "But what if I'm faced with an emergency?" The Bible tells us to expect problems. Jesus says, "In this world you will have trouble." Not we *might* have trouble, but we *will* have trouble. Yet, aren't we surprised when our car breaks down or when we are confronted with an unexpected illness or when Christmas comes? Not planning for the unexpected, we turn to our credit cards. Since I know there will be emergencies, I try to plan for them by setting aside an emergency fund. What that doesn't cover, I trust God to handle.

□ "But what if I need to make hotel or airline reservations—don't I need a credit card for that?" With the advent of debit cards, we no longer need credit cards for reserving a room or a flight. Most banks now offer debit card holders the same protection as credit card holders.

□ "But what if a business won't take payment by debit card?" If a place does not accept a debit card, then my business goes elsewhere. Simple as that.

You may disagree about eliminating all of your credit cards, but I challenge you to consider keeping only one. De-clutter your wallet. Start setting aside money so you so don't have to rely on plastic.

## Live in a "Cash Only" Society

What does living by "cash only" look like?

- □ Pay cash instead of writing a check when we grab a coffee at Starbucks.
- □ Use cash rather than a debit card to buy groceries.
- □ Hand the cashier greenbacks from your wallet rather than a credit card when purchasing clothes.

Just because the rest of the world pays for normal expenses by check or plastic, doesn't require us to follow suit. Psychologically, it hurts us more to spend cash than it does to write a check or use debit or credit. If we pay by cash, we buy less stuff.

## Establish a Budget

Allocating a certain amount of money for weekly expenses prevents us from spending more money on things we don't really need. If I'm left with no entertainment money after going out for dinner and a movie, then I skip my latte at the coffee shop. I won't buy those party supplies if there's not enough in my grocery budget when I already have plain paper plates at home.

## Practice "Just-in-Time Buying"

I once thought buying stuff in advance of when I needed it would save me lots of money. I was known for buying Christmas gifts several months ahead of time as I discovered great bargains on gift items throughout the year. Then one day I realized I was not saving money, and those presents cluttered up my home.

- □ I misplaced gifts and ended up buying replacement presents.
- □ I simply found more stuff to buy and gave more.
- □ I changed my mind about gifts, bought something else, but kept the original gifts.
- □ I had to buy different gifts because the recipients no longer wanted or needed the items because I bought their presents too early.

Do we really want to add the extra work of tracking all the receipts from items we bought months in advance? Will these stores even provide refunds if they need to be returned months after they were purchased? If we are having issues with clutter, is it a wise decision to store gifts or buy personal items months ahead of time?

But I didn't stop at gifts. There's more. And all this stuff cost money and required storage space in my home. I used to stock my pantry so full that you'd think we weren't going to be near a grocery store for a year. When I was pregnant, I started collecting home-schooling materials up to the fifth grade level. Family members helped me pack my baby's closet so full that he had clothes that would fit him when he started kindergarten.

And let me tell you about my books. It was my dream to own a personal library. Hundreds—and I do mean hundreds—of books piled on bookshelves, in closets, boxes, and on the floors waited patiently for me to rescue them. I bought them, planning to read each one someday. But there were just too many books and not enough time to sort through them to find the one particular book on my latest topic of interest. So I bought the same one again.

How about you? What do you collect? What do you stash around the house to use someday?

Evaluate how much it's costing you to buy Christmas gifts in July. Even though you bought cards in January at 75 percent off, are you buying new ones again in November? How long are you stashing those party supplies to use someday? Are you buying duplicate scrapbook supplies because you can't find the ones you purchased eight months ago?

There's a freedom in buying what you need when you need it. Nothing gets lost or damaged. You don't have to stress about losing the receipt if you need to return it. There's no reason to worry if the store will even accept the return one year after the purchase. You're not buying extra because you found the same item in a different style you like better. Duplicates and triplicates of things aren't invading your home because you can't locate the original. You don't have to worry about your brother buying himself a fishing rod just like the one you bought to give him next Christmas.

Not only does "just-in-time buying" save you extra money, it saves you from extra clutter!

## Stop Cutting Coupons

Stop cutting coupons to save money—can that be right? It sure is! Coupons are mini-advertisements to market products we would not ordinarily buy. Some people with loads of discipline can save money with coupons. Clutterbugs tend not to fall in this category. We cut coupons and forget about them. When we use them, we often purchase things that would not have made it on the grocery list without the coupon. They are enticements to buy more stuff. And if we don't use them, the coupons clutter our homes.

## Create a Penny Jar

Loose change. Yes, even coins are clutter when they're scattered about the house. Use a piggy bank, mason jar, or other container as a home for spare change. Do not include this money in your monthly budget. Save it until the jar is full. Then treat yourself to something special. Preferably something that won't clutter your home, like a massage or a new hairstyle.

## Avoid Debt at All Costs

Finance plans, student loans, car loans, personal loans—any type of borrowing—clutters our homes with more stuff, our mailboxes with more bills, our schedules with more headaches, and our relationships with more stress.

Why do we buy new automobiles that lose 30 to 40 percent of their value and then pay interest on them for another four or five years? Even on a used automobile—if we have to borrow money, then maybe we need to consider the fact that we just can't afford it. Think about the emotional clutter from that big car payment every month.

Also, we don't have to buy things simply because we can afford the cost. My husband, yearning for a big, European, military truck called a Unimog, urged me to borrow money to buy one. I told him that if he wanted a Unimog, we needed to save up the money. So we did, and now we have a big, old, ugly Unimog cluttering our driveway. He doesn't really use it, but he likes to look at it and admire it.

Moving on to personal loans—they are the worst. My husband and I borrowed $2,000 from my in-laws to use toward our first house. It created tension between us—and that was certainly not their fault. It was just that I didn't like owing money to them. I felt indebted to my in-laws. That added some relational clutter I didn't need.

So what about mortgages? Is that debt OK? It's more accurate to call it tolerable. Since we either have to pay rent or mortgage, at least with a mortgage the payments eventually end. But we can shoot for smaller monthly payments in a smaller house. Less square footage equals lower heating costs. Less money is spent on decorating and landscaping. A smaller house means less to clean. Above all, smaller homes hold less clutter.

## DEBT AND CLUTTER

Let's dig deeper in the relationship between debt and clutter. It takes money to buy the things that end up littering our homes. We charge more stuff on our credit cards that will become clutter. Then we keep paying for our junk because it costs money to maintain it, insure it, clean it, and store it. Our pocketbooks get thinner and our homes grow fatter.

And then there's the incidental clutter associated with debt. Each monthly bill brings more papers to track. Credit card receipts cram our wallets. Billing statements end up scattered throughout our homes, some with payment checks inside them. We open new store accounts to save that extra 10 percent, but pay more in finance charges and late fees down the road.

Debt clogs our minds. We stress over the money we owe. We think about our payment deadline and if we'll have enough money to cover the minimum monthly payment.

Debt steals our time. We waste hours shopping sales and charging stuff we really can't afford. Then we spend time writing out checks for each credit card bill. More check writing means more time for balancing our checkbooks. Then, when we don't pay promptly, we lose chunks of our days responding to collectors.

Debt eats away at our relationships. Relationships deteriorate from arguing over spending habits, including the stuff we bought and the things we want to buy. We even find ourselves fighting over the clutter in our homes caused by warehousing items we are still paying for. We don't enjoy living surrounded by clutter. But we love our possessions too much to give them away, throw them away, or sell them. So our debts increase as we finance all of our heart's desires, and our relationships pay the toll.

Debt. It clutters our homes, minds, schedules, and even our relationships. If you have debt, get rid of it. If you are free of it, stay away from it.

### HOMEBUILDING

*Keep your lives free from the love of money and be content with what you have, because God has said, "Never will I leave you; never will I forsake you"* (Heb. 13:5).

How eager are you to attain more and more stuff? Are your pocketbooks pierced with a grief called debt? Or have you embraced a lifestyle of contentment?

Start praying for contentment. Trust in the Lord to fulfill your needs. Stop depending on plastic and start relying on God.

### De-Cluttering My Heart

Lord, forgive me for:

Lord, thank You for:

Lord, help me with:

## De-Cluttering My Home

What steps can I take to live within my means?

How can I adjust my gift-buying habits to reduce the flow of clutter in my home?

How do I plan to pay off debt? What habits do I need to change to become a better money manager?

# 15 THE CLEAN DREAM

**"REMEMBER** you can only stay organized once you accept that less is more. Less clutter equals less cleaning time, less frustration, and more space and enjoyment for you and your family."[16]

My sister's house was once buried under toys. After making major strides in de-cluttering her home, friends and family expressed delight in the progress she made. But they also uttered a few comments hinting she still had a ways to go.

"You did a great job picking up all the toys, Pam. But you know, it wouldn't hurt to take out the vacuum now that the floor is clear."

"Wow! Look at this kitchen! I can see you've been working hard. Maybe you could wipe down the counters too!"

"Where did all the clutter that was on the kitchen table go? I'm so proud of you. Oh look, you forgot to take a rag and actually clean the table."

Funny that none of these people offered to help my sister with the cleaning after she de-cluttered, but such is life. It was a needed wake-up call to point out that the job isn't finished when the de-cluttering is done.

When I asked my sister how she missed vacuuming the floor, wiping the counters, and cleaning the table, she explained that she didn't see that dirt. After living for so long in a messy home, clearing out the junk made it appear like a palace to her.

My sister explains, "To me, extreme mess is normal. That is

what I grew up with. When I pick up all the clutter, it looks clean to me." She, too, struggled with keeping a clean house. When I left for college, my sister still had another decade of living in a house that would continue to grow messier.

This story prompts the questions, "How do we know when our homes are clean?" and "How clean is clean enough?"

When I first began my quest for a clean home, I asked my friends who kept beautiful-looking homes to share their secrets. What formula did they use? Did they hire maids? How often did they clean? But I was disappointed in the answers. They generally responded, "I clean when my house needs to be cleaned." What kind of answer is that? That's not helpful! So the conversation continued:

"How do you know when something needs to be cleaned?"

"When it's dirty."

"But don't you keep some sort of schedule?"

"Not really."

*I was getting nowhere fast.* "Then tell me how often you vacuum."

"Once a day, or maybe every couple days. It depends on what the carpet looks like."

"What about sweeping and mopping the kitchen floor?"

"I probably sweep once a day and mop once a week, but I do it more often if the floors need it."

*Aha. Maybe I was onto something.* "So you do keep a schedule!"

"I don't call it a schedule. I see that something needs to be cleaned, and I clean it."

When I asked my friends about cleaning, a pattern emerged, indicating a schedule. Yet they refused to acknowledge using a system. I later learned they did have a system—based on standards. They each went by a personal definition of clean. When that standard wasn't met, it was time to clean.

It took me a long time to comprehend this. Everything I read told me I needed some kind of system that involved scheduling housework. Many books recommended writing my chores on 3 x 5 cards. That didn't work because my index cards got lost in the clutter. Then there was zone cleaning, but that was just too diffi-cult to follow for my simple mind. Other books suggested clean-ing 15 minutes a day. That would be wonderful if my home was reasonably clean to begin with. Sure, I could maintain my messy home with a few minutes of housework each day, but how could I do better?

So what's a clutterbug to do? Nothing seemed to work for me. When I tried cleaning only when something looked dirty, I failed miserably. I missed areas or forgot entire sections. Over-whelmed by all the catch-up work necessary to make the house appear tidy, I felt defeated.

Establishing a schedule sounded a little easier. I liked the idea of using a checklist to remind me what chores needed to be done. But if something wasn't on the schedule, it stayed dirty. And with all the de-cluttering yet to be done, I couldn't keep up with the list of chores.

The marriage of cleaning by standards and cleaning by schedule provided the ultimate solution. I decided what my standards of clean are. Once I defined specific standards, they became my goals. I knew I couldn't achieve my vision of clean in a day, especially with all the de-cluttering yet to be done, so I set up a schedule of daily, weekly, monthly, and annual chores. The schedule is more like a checklist. I do what I can and start fresh the next day. I call this combination of standards and schedule my cleaning plan.

What are your standards of clean? Determine what is accept-able and write it down. Is a soap ring by the sink OK until you get to it on your schedule? Can you live with fingerprints on the fridge? How much grease can you handle on the hood over the stove?

Have you developed a cleaning routine? Do you know what chores need to be completed daily and which ones are OK to skip if you don't get to them? Write a chore list and decide how often each chore needs to be performed. When you notice some-thing doesn't meet your definition of clean, take care of it. Even if it is not on the schedule.

Think about how specific you want to get. Many of the routines I initially tried to implement were too general, like "clean the bathroom." But what does it really mean to clean the bathroom? Is it just cleaning the toilet? Or is it mopping the floor, wiping the counters, and scrubbing the tub? And do I have to do all each day?

To create my cleaning plan, I wrote it so that a child could look at it and know what needs to be done. When something on my cleaning plan didn't work, I changed it around. I kept a checklist—a list of daily chores gives me a sense of accomplishment when I cross each chore off. When I realized zone cleaning didn't work for me, I tried grouping similar weekly chores together—that works better for me.

Use my plan as a template to develop your own system. Feel free to modify this to fit your cleaning needs. If you own live plants, add watering plants to the list. If you have pets, especially ones that shed, some of the weekly chores may need to be moved to daily chores.

## Daily Chores

- ☐ Make the bed.
- ☐ Wash the dishes. Clean the kitchen sink, including the faucet. (If it means plates will stack up in the sink just because there's space for a few more glasses, then don't wait until the dishwasher is completely full.)
- ☐ Clear new clutter off countertops and tables.
- ☐ Wipe countertops and tables.
- ☐ Sweep the kitchen floor.
- ☐ Clean the toilet, inside and out.
- ☐ Clear new clutter from bathroom counters. Clean the sink, including faucet.
- ☐ Pick clothes up from the bathroom floor and do a quick wipe-down of the floor with wet bathroom tissue.
- ☐ Do a minimum of one load of laundry. (This includes emptying the dryer, folding clothes, putting them away, and cleaning the lint filter for the next load.)
- ☐ Check wastebaskets, take out trash if three-quarters full or more.

□ Take a trash walk. Stroll around the house with an empty grocery bag in hand, looking for debris that needs to be picked up.

□ Take a clutter walk. Stroll around the house looking for things out of place and take them back to their rightful homes.

□ Take care of anything that does not meet your standards of clean as you come across it.

## Weekly Chores

Day 1

□ Mop floors and vacuum carpets.

□ Clean mats and throw rugs.

Day 2

□ Change bed linens.

Day 3

□ Clean outsides of appliances.

□ Clean mirrors.

□ Scour tub.

Day 4

□ Clean doorknobs and door handles.

□ Clean switch plates.

□ Clean telephones.

Day 5

□ Brush animals.

□ Empty all the trash. (Assign this chore for the evening before your regularly scheduled trash pickup.) Place a few extra bags in the bottom of wastebaskets so that a fresh bag is available when you empty the trash during the week.

Day 6

□ Work on monthly chores.

## Monthly Chores

Week 1

□ Clean inside the refrigerator, microwave, stove (and stove hood), and other appliances.

- □ Wash out wastebaskets.
- □ Clean outside of cabinets.
- □ Clean under the kitchen and bathroom sinks.

Week 2

- □ Clean baseboards.
- □ Clear clutter from tops of washer and dryer, then wipe tops of washer and dryer.
- □ Pull out appliances and furniture to clean underneath and behind them with mop or vacuum.
- □ Clean under the bed.

Week 3

- □ Clean windows and inside window panes.
- □ Check walls and doors for scuff marks, cleaning where needed.
- □ Dust furniture.
- □ Dust lighting fixtures.

Week 4

- □ Groom pets.
- □ Check cabinets, drawers, and closets for new clutter and straighten them up. Wash tray or basket where silverware is kept.
- □ Clean purse.
- □ Clean car.

## Annual Chores

Fit these in throughout the year or in one big burst during spring cleaning season:

- □ Call professional cleaners to steam-clean carpets and furniture, letting them clean the ducts as well. Pay the extra few dollars for a Teflon coat on the carpet—it is well worth it.
- □ Clean drapes and curtains.
- □ Clean coils underneath refrigerator.
- □ Clean garage and other major storage areas such as spare rooms, attics, and basements.
- □ Thin out filing cabinets, pulling out any papers no longer necessary to keep.

☐ Perform a room-by-room de-cluttering spree, doing a different room each month.

If something is already clean when you get to it on your list, skip it. If there's nothing in the trash, would you take out an empty bag? Then, why wash the windows when they look great to begin with?

Be smart when deciding if you can hold off on a chore until the next time around. Places like kitchens and bathrooms still hide bacteria when they look clean. Bed sheets may appear fresh, but then again, you can't see those microscopic mites.

Don't sweat not following your cleaning plan to a tee. If you never had one before, it may take a while to establish new cleaning habits. Focus on what you're able to do rather than what you missed. Incorporate the amount of chores you can handle while de-cluttering. Add a little more each week.

Think of learning how to keep a clean house like an infant learning to walk. It takes about a year for babies to develop leg muscles strong enough for them to stand on their own. It takes time for cleaning habits to become ingrained in our daily routine.

When children stand by themselves for the first time, we cheer them on. When they tumble while trying to take those first steps, we encourage them to keep going. And before we know it, little feet scamper all over the house, running every which way as if they walked from birth. Learning to keep a clean home is similar. In the beginning, you may need someone to hold your hands. When people encourage us, they motivate us to take another step. Sometimes we will tumble. But we get back up and keep on trying.

Set a goal for yourself. Every day do one thing to make your house look a little nicer than the day before. Take small baby steps each day. Seek progress, not perfection.

### HOMEBUILDING

*Search me, O God, and know my heart; test me and know my anxious thoughts. See if there is any offensive way in me, and lead me in the way everlasting* (Ps. 139:23-24).

How clean is your heart? None of us is perfect, so we all have a little work to do here. Good thing none of our friends can give a white-glove test on our hearts. But God knows what's in there, and He wants to help with the de-cluttering.

It's been said that God makes His home in our hearts. Let's do a little heart cleaning. Let go of what doesn't need to be there, like bitterness, unforgiveness, worry, and greed. Ask God to remove these things and replace them with joy, forgiveness, trust, and contentment. Confess what needs God's forgiveness that He may create in you a cleansed heart. And like cleaning your house, make a habit of daily heart cleaning.

## De-Cluttering My Heart

Lord, forgive me for:

Lord, thank You for:

Lord, help me with:

## De-Cluttering My Home

What cleaning methods have I tried in the past? From previous experience, what worked and what didn't work?

What chore do I like least? Have I tried using a cleaning buddy, playing music, or testing different cleaning supplies? How can I make it more enjoyable?

What chore do I like the most? Why?

# 16 CREATIVE DE-CLUTTERING

**"'ORGANIZED'** is not a destination, but a journey. It's not about perfectionism, but progress."[17]

Are you ready to have some fun de-cluttering? Cleaning will never be the same once you implement some of the creative techniques below:

## SACRED COW HUNTING

In the business world, a sacred cow refers to an outdated practice that inhibits positive change. In homemaking, sacred cows prevent the transformation of our messy houses into presentable homes. They're the items we keep due to faulty thinking. We tell ourselves, "That's the way we've always done it," or "That's something we've always owned."

Go on a sacred cow hunt. Look for things you normally wouldn't consider parting with. Evaluate if these prized possessions are truly worth keeping.

Ask questions like:

- □ What was the original reason for obtaining this item?
- □ Why am I keeping it?
- □ Is it still used for its intended purpose? Why or why not?
- □ Do I enjoy using it? Why or why not?
- □ Do I treat it in a respectful manner? How does the way I store or display it show that I value it?
- □ What would happen if I threw it away?

□ How do I feel about keeping it?

Based on your answers, objectively decide what you want to do with it.

Practice sacred cow hunting with me. Let's look at holiday storage. Hmmm . . . I see a Christmas tree. I certainly can't part with that, right? Well, let's ask the questions anyway.

□ *What was the original reason for buying my Christmas tree?* So I could use it to celebrate Christmas.

□ *Why am I keeping this?* Because it is a tradition in my family to celebrate Christmas with a tree. I like the way it makes the house look festive during the holidays.

□ *Is the tree still used for its intended purpose? Why or why not?* Yes. I put it up every year because I own it. Owning it obligates me to use it. Plus, that's the way we've always celebrated Christmas.

□ *Do I enjoy using it? Why or why not?* Putting up the tree and taking it down has become a burden. I no longer enjoy this because no one else is interested in helping me with it. I dislike taking off ornaments, putting them back in their boxes, and storing them for another year. I still enjoy putting presents under the tree and relaxing to soft Christmas music in a dim room lit by tree lights.

□ *Do I treat this item in a respectful manner? How does the way I display or store it show that I value it?* I take the time to decorate the tree to make it look pleasing. I pack the tree back in its box. I haphazardly toss ornaments, lights, and other decorations into a storage box.

□ *What would happen if I threw it away and celebrated without a tree?* If I didn't have a tree, I wouldn't have to spend time putting it up, decorating it, and taking it down. Without the tree, I can lose the extra Christmas lights, ornaments, garland, and ribbon. No tree means fewer decorations, less clutter, and less stuff to store. I can still celebrate Christmas with a real tree or even a potted miniature pine.

□ *How do I feel about keeping it?* Based on my answers, I will no longer keep an artificial tree and most of the decorations that go along with it. Instead, I will try a new tradition of celebrating Christmas with a real tree. If I discover that a real tree is too much work or that I like the artificial tree better, I can always buy a new one during those 75-percent-off sales after Christmas. I will only keep the decorations I absolutely love.

(The above sacred cow hunt actually happened in my home. I love not having to bother with an artificial tree!)

## CLEAN SWEEP HOME EDITION

Do you ever watch the show *Clean Sweep* on The Learning Channel (TLC)? Why not perform your own modified version of the show?

Mimic TLC's famous program without the cameras, personal carpenters, designers, and professional organizers. Get a team of friends to help you move everything out of one or two rooms in your house. Create a keep pile, toss pile, and sale pile.

Do a quick 20-minute sort of everything. Move as much as you can into either the sale pile or toss pile. Any questionable items go in the keep pile to evaluate during the major sort.

Perform the major sort, establishing a new keep pile. Be conscientious of the room size and what will reasonably fit back in there.

Hold a big yard sale. Price the items to sell. Anything not sold goes immediately to a local charity. No storing things in the garage for another yard sale next week.

I performed a clean sweep like this at my sister's house. She had a sunroom, basement, and garage full of storage. People asked us if we were moving because it looked like everything she owned sat in the front yard—extra furniture, decorations, dishes, books, toys, clothes, you name it. We priced things to sell and made a modest profit. But the best part of it was all the extra space this created in her house.

## FREEBIE GIVEAWAY

Instead of a lawn sale, have a freebie giveaway. Tell people they must take items by the box. No picking through things. Later, they can donate or sell what they don't want.

This is one that I love to do. You can get rid of a lot in a short period of time. When I did the big yard sale with my sister, we had a huge freebie pile filled with things that would not fetch a decent price. When the yard sale ended, everything went to the freebie pile. People looking for free stuff saved us the trouble of making several trips to haul away leftovers to a donation center.

## "CLUTTERSIZE"

Ever heard of Jazzersize—exercise using jazz moves to music? Well, cluttersizing is exercise by de-cluttering to music. Find a favorite adrenaline pumping music CD. Play it while de-cluttering. This works best when doing it with friends.

## HOME REPO STORE

Not sure what to do with all the stuff lying around the house belonging to other family members? Create a home repo store! Put other people's belongings in a box to be "sold" once a week or once a month. Select specific hours to open the home repo store. Family members are responsible for reclaiming their repossessed items. Offer the owner their belongings for sale at a flat rate of 25 cents or even $1.00. If they choose not to come get them, they lose them. Be gracious, lest you find family members adding your stuff to the home repo store.

Modify the store guidelines to fit your needs. When I did this with my husband, we didn't charge each other to get things back. We used it as a tool to discipline ourselves to pick up our stuff in a timely manner.

## DE-CLUTTERING OLYMPICS

One of the questions I frequently hear in my circle of mom friends is how to get kids motivated to clean. Most children and adults have a competitive nature. Why not bring out some competition for cleaning house?

Set aside a weekend for your own De-Cluttering Olympics. All family members must participate. Offer prizes for different categories such as:

- □ Cleanest room
- □ Most items tossed
- □ Fastest de-clutterer
- □ Outstanding sportsmanship (for helping other family members clean and de-clutter)

To make it fun for all participants, create an award category for everyone. Choose prizes that will not add clutter to the home. Take children to their favorite restaurant, a family arcade, or maybe miniature golfing. Give older kids gift certificates to a movie or tickets to a sporting event. Treat your spouse to a massage or a special dinner. Or offer verbal praise.

## CLEANING PARTY

Some people host tea parties, others throw painting parties and moving parties. Why not a cleaning party? Invite a few friends over to help with the cleaning. Keep plenty of beverages on hand, including bottled water. Have snacks available—the kind that won't make a lot of crumbs.

When I fall behind on the housekeeping, having a few gal pals over to help always energizes me. Sometimes, they just visit while I clean. All they need to do is sit at the kitchen table and chat with me while I superclean the fridge or mop the floor.

## THE MINIMIZER

Look for collections around the house and think of ways to shrink them. Here are some ideas:

- □ Take pictures of all those trophies from Little League. Put the photos in a scrapbook and toss the trophies.
- □ Not ready to part with a T-shirt collection styling clever sayings? Hire someone to make them into a quilt.
- □ Remove patches from old scouting uniforms. Get rid of the uniforms and use the patches to make a shadowbox.

My husband minimized his tool collection by selling some of

the bulky ones in return for me chipping in to pay for newer, slimmer, all-purpose versions.

## GENERAL CONTRACTOR

Hire professionals to help you create the look you desire. Employ a cleaning lady to assist in scrubbing down the house. Call a professional organizer to help you with sorting and organizing. Consult with an interior designer for decorating your home.

About once a year, I treat myself to a cleaning lady. It's just nice to have a break now and then. Depending on our finances, I decide if I want to subcontract everything or just the least appealing chores.

## KRIS KRINGLE

Remember back in school being someone's secret gift giver? Play Kris Kringle as an adult by regifting brand-new items cluttering the home. But don't wait for Christmas. Let the season of goodwill begin today!

Give items to your church ministries—they make great giveaways for special events. Surprise a new mom by giving her the baby clothes your little one never wore. Give a book you're not interested in to a friend who will love it.

## TOP 10 LIST

Scavenge the house for the top 10 clutter collections. Every family member participates by creating his or her own list. Meet together and compare what each person found. Collections noticed by everybody become the priority clutter hot spots to be worked on that day. The following day, each family member creates another list, the top 10 progress spots. This gives everyone the opportunity to give encouragement and receive positive feedback.

I like doing top 10 lists because they help me prioritize where I need to focus my attention. When my husband makes these lists with me, I know we are on the same page. We don't feel like we're nagging each other because together we evaluate areas in which to focus our de-cluttering efforts.

# HOME CLEANING SUMMIT

Decide cleaning and de-cluttering expectations as a family. Individuals take ownership in this process by being given a voice. Ask each family member:

☐ What would you like to see the house look like?

☐ What are you willing to do to reach and maintain that vision?

☐ What standards of clean would you like to define for our home?

Use this time to create a cleaning schedule and chore chart. Select a date to evaluate the housekeeping effectiveness. Consider holding monthly summits to discuss cleaning and de-cluttering issues.

In my household, we have weekly family conferences in which we discuss our schedules, current projects, and things we'd like to do. We incorporate an informal version of a home cleaning summit into these meetings.

We also do 10 minutes of daily couch time together. During these mini-meetings we share what we did during the day (not just what we cleaned), remind one another of the evening's schedule, and ask for help with anything that still needs to get done. This is our time to touch base with one another and take the family pulse.

Think about how you can meet with your family to discuss what's on your mind while giving others a chance to say their piece. Homemaking is not just about keeping a clean house. As home managers we need to communicate with our families. We need to practice dialogues, not monologues. Family time creates incredible opportunities to bring your spouse and children together as a team to make a beautiful home together.

## HOMEBUILDING

*Consider it pure joy, my brothers, whenever you face trials of many kinds, because you know that the testing of your faith develops perseverance. Perseverance must finish its work so that you may be mature and complete, not lacking anything* (James 1:2-4).

We may not immediately think of housework as pure joy, but why not give it a try? Develop a positive attitude because Christ is at work within us. Just like our homes are a work in progress, so are we.

## De-Cluttering My Heart

Lord, forgive me for:

Lord, thank You for:

Lord, help me with:

## De-Cluttering My Home

Where might I begin hunting for sacred cows in my home?

What are some of the collections I can reduce in size? How might I go about minimizing them?

In what ways can I make de-cluttering more fun? How might my family like to participate?

# EPILOGUE
## THE DIRT ON ME

**"MESSIES** are generally wonderful people. Just between you and me, I think they are a cut above the average. They are creative, intelligent, nice people."[18]

"I hear you live in a messy house!" my childhood playmate accused. "Is that true?" Her eyes squinted in anger. Her condemning voice rang through my ears.

"No," I lied, "that's not true."

While other neighborhood children invited playmates inside their homes, no friends were allowed inside my house. And after that confrontation, I feared what anyone would say who stepped through our front door.

### TOO MUCH STUFF

By the time I reached elementary school, I mastered the art of *mess* and fully embraced the *too much stuff* lifestyle. To say I kept a messy bedroom would be an understatement. But I also commandeered the "quick clean" technique. If threatened with losing playtime, I simply kicked all the stuff on my floor under the bed.

I never felt I had enough stuff, always wanting more. It felt like I had so little. There were too many toys to play with, but not much of value. I had lots of clothes, but only a few nice outfits. Plenty of electronics, jewelry, stationery, books, games, but what did I have to show for it? Lack of organizational skills. Lost and broken items. No discipline.

As I grew older, toys, papers, clothes, and other collections increased. Likewise, the available space between my floor and box spring decreased, forcing me to find a new place to put all my things.

□ □ □

"You will stay inside this house all weekend unless you clean your room!" my mother scolded.

"No problem!" I slyly replied. This 10-year old had a plan.

A couple of hours later, I informed my mother that I finished cleaning my room.

"I need to inspect it first," she responded in disbelief. After all, how could I have cleaned such a big mess in so short a time?

Mother slowly made her way upstairs to my bedroom. Her eyes nearly popped out of their sockets. Astonished with my thorough cleaning job, she stared at the clear floor, my neatly made bed, and clutter-free dresser tops.

"Wow! It looks good!" she said as her eyes scanned the room. Then she paused for a moment and glanced back at the bed. "You shoved everything under the bed, didn't you?" Expecting to catch me cheating, she stooped to her knees and checked. "Well, where did you put everything?"

"It's put away," I replied.

Mother walked toward the closet door.

*Uh oh*, I thought, *I hope she doesn't check inside there.*

As Mother turned the handle, I held my breath, preparing for her reaction. Clothes, toys, electronics, along with other odds and ends tumbled out of my stuffed closet. Jam-packed from floor to ceiling, this avalanche of things cascaded down, spoiling my clear floor.

Red-faced, my mother yelled, "You will clean this up *now!* And you're grounded!"

I shoved many of the fallen items under the bed, stuffed what was left back in the closet, and pulled out my extra-large, adult travel suitcase holding more than 50 Barbies and all their accessories. *Playtime!*

□ □ □

Living in a messy home has the potential to cause physical harm too.

My school drama club cast me in the role of Violet in *Charlie and the Chocolate Factory.* I wanted to be Veruca, the bad egg. I related to her. She wanted everything, and she wanted it all now.

One day after play practice, a bee buzzed around my head. I dashed inside the house with the bee in hot pursuit. The buzz sounded like it was circling me once inside the doorway. I felt like a helpless swimmer surrounded by sharks. I ran to the living room and tripped over a book as I fled for safety.

My ankle swelled to the size of a baseball. A visit to the doctor revealed I separated a growth plate. Required to wear a cast, I limped on crutches for six weeks. And my acting career ended. Just like that.

I looked for someone to blame. But the book lying on the floor was part of the encyclopedia set I used earlier in the week to write a report for class.

## CLEANING REFLECTIONS

As a child, my cleaning contributions were minimal, but my clutter donations remained quite generous. I rarely threw things away, often received lots of stuff, and consistently overvalued possessions. And all the time, I believed that none of the mess was my fault.

When my mother instructed me to pick up my toys, I refused (unless coerced with threats). When she told me to clean my room, I snapped back, "Only if you clean yours first!" I certainly avoided chores she attempted to delegate to me. After all, why should I be required to clean when my mother didn't pick up the house to my expectations? She should be the one setting the example, right?

Admittedly, I was a spoiled, rotten brat. But I did have a heart. There were times when I tried to help, even wanted to help, but more often I found better things to do than clean. Like staring at the leaves falling off the trees outside, watching the dog sleep, or doing homework. In fact, a root canal sounded like more fun than picking up all the stuff lying around the house.

And then there was dinnertime. Dining at home proved to

be a disaster we all wanted to avoid. Dishes were usually piled high in the kitchen sink, and nobody wanted to tackle that job. Eating out was the rule, not the exception.

Did I ever offer to wash the dishes? Nope, not that I can remember. Besides, that was Mom's job. Why would I want to volunteer for it? Until the dishes were clean again, I didn't mind using paper plates and plastic utensils.

I didn't view housekeeping as my responsibility, but I did help dirty the dishes, I added to the laundry, and I left toys on the floor. My shoes brought dust, leaves, pebbles, mud, and slush in from the yard. I left fingerprints on the counters and door handles. But no, I did not help clean the house. I placed all of the blame on my mother. Not realizing I was responsible for *some* of the mess, I let my mother take responsibility for *all* of the mess.

When I was 15 years old, I finally decided to clean the living room while my mother went shopping one afternoon. I wanted to start there because everybody used that room, and it was the messiest place in our home.

Newspapers and magazines cluttered the outskirts of the living room floor. A layer of dog hair was plastered to the carpet. Mounds of laundry waited on the couches to be folded. Scattered toys lay forgotten in every corner. Every shelf and end table bore the weight of too much stuff.

I bagged up the expired coupons, old newspapers, food wrappers, and other trash. Anything my mother needed to sort through, I put in boxes.

Upon her return home, my mother expressed her displeasure at me for messing up *her* room. "What have you done? Why did you touch my things?" Spying the expired coupons in the trash bags, she screamed, "Why did you throw them out? There could be one I can still use!"

She dumped the bags of trash right in the middle of the clean floor. Any flicker of desire to help with housework was buried under that mess.

Later I realized my mother's attachment to stuff went beyond what I misjudged as laziness. Her issues were beyond the understanding of a teenager. All I felt then was that the trash was more important to her than I was.

Yearning for peace and a sense of order, the disarray engulfed me like a tornado. Home never became a haven to run to—it was a whirlwind of mess and clutter to run away from.

To be sure, I experienced happy times with my family. But piles and boxes and bags of clutter overshadow many of the joyful memories.

## MAKING PEACE

Looking back, I recognize that my mother's problem of too much stuff was symptomatic of far deeper issues related to depression and hoarding. Back in the 1980s, obsessive-compulsive hoarding disorder (OCHD) was virtually unheard of. Today, hoarding to the point of impaired living conditions is recognized as a serious illness by a growing number of professionals in the mental health arena.

My mother didn't want to live in a messy house. She often expressed her desire for something better. I remember watching her do laundry or wash dishes, but the work seemed to pile up faster than she could keep up with it. And more stuff flowing into the house put her even further behind. Hours of catch-up cleaning only proved how much more needed to be done. In my mother's world, the cleaning was never finished.

As an adult, I developed a good relationship with my mother—despite the cluttered home in which I grew up. In the end, she did help me learn to keep a clean house. She taught me by example that:

□ Dishes left to a "fairy godwasher" linger dirty in the sink.
□ Shelves covered with armies of knickknacks are difficult to dust.
□ Holding on to unneeded clothing creates mountains of laundry.

I do not blame my mother for what she didn't teach me but am grateful for what I learned.

## A NEW DAY

My growing-up years taught me some hard lessons. I lived in a messy house and kept a messy bedroom; I thought cleaning would come naturally once I moved out on my own. But I continued to find excuse after excuse for not cleaning:

"I don't have the time. I'm just too busy."

"My husband (or job or schoolwork) is too demanding."

"If I had more storage bins, I could get this place clean."

Excuses aside, the real reason was that the clutter was always in the way. I had too much stuff.

Finally, I asked myself, "Am I willing to give up the clutter for a clean house?" I loved my stuff, but not enough to continue sacrificing my quality of life. In return for a presentable home, I gave up the clutter.

Surprisingly, de-cluttering didn't feel like hard work because once I got started, I experienced how fun it was to let go of things. It took me a year of consistent de-cluttering until my home reached a manageable point. Here's what that looks like:

- ☐ Flat surfaces generally remain clear of clutter. Important documents no longer get lost in a sea of stuff.
- ☐ People don't walk into my home and wonder if I just moved in because of boxes stacked against walls in every room.
- ☐ Closets hold items in a reasonably organized fashion. Frustration levels decreased because I don't have to go on a scavenger hunt to locate the valuables stashed on crowded shelves piled with junk.
- ☐ The food in my pantry gets used. No more buying duplicates of things I can't find.
- ☐ My bedroom is not overrun by laundry. The clothes in my dresser actually fit and look good on me.

Gone are the days of clinging to every so-called sacred treasure—junk that wasn't even garage-sale caliber. No more shoving things under my bed and cramming stuff in closets. Throwing the clutter out brings me extreme joy!

Today, homemaking is an expression of love, not a dreaded

task. I once avoided dirty dishes like the plague they might have carried. Now, I enjoy the sight of clean and neatly stacked plates in my cupboard. Sure, there are days I still struggle to stay on top of things, but I'm no longer overwhelmed by the thought of housecleaning. I feel confident in my ability to create a nice home for my family.

And people see me differently these days. They tell me I'm more relationship focused. Instead of spending so much time shopping and tending to all my stuff, friends notice me making time for them. Plus, my communication skills have improved without the distractions from images of clutter lurking in the back of my mind.

So how did I break free from the chains of possession overload? Was it years of therapy? A magic medication? A reality-TV-show home makeover? No. My desire for stuff dwindled after I learned to trust in God in areas where I didn't know faith issues existed.

A slave to my collections of junk, my possessions owned me. I never realized I was in bondage to clutter. On my own, there's no way I could have let go of my passion for too much stuff. When I asked God to reclaim the area in my heart consumed by clutter, I began to trust in Him instead of trusting in stuff:

- □ I don't have to stockpile a year's worth of food. If I'm ever caught with an empty pantry in a natural or man-made disaster, I know my family will be just fine. God will provide.
- □ It won't be the end of the world if prices go up. I'm not worried about not having enough money. God will give me the resources and take care of my needs.
- □ I don't feel compelled to hold onto things "just in case." When "just in case" happens, God will be there.

God taught me to depend on Him as He gave me the people, resources, and strength to de-junk my heart and home. With every prayer, my tight-fisted grasp to the junk in my home loosened. I stopped wanting more and became content with less. Through Him, I am freed from a lifestyle of too much stuff.

### HOMEBUILDING

*Now to him who is able to do immeasurably more than all we ask or imagine, according to his power that is at work within us, to him be glory in the church and in Christ Jesus throughout all generations, for ever and ever! Amen (Eph. 3:20-22).*

When God is at work within us, let's give Him the glory. *Thank You, Lord, for transforming my heart and home. Amen.*

## De-Cluttering My Heart

Lord, forgive me for:

Lord, thank You for:

Lord, help me with:

## De-Cluttering My Home

In what areas do I need to start accepting responsibility? Where can I do a better job?

Do I need to make peace with people or events from my past? What steps can I take to begin that process today?

How can God free me from the too-much-stuff lifestyle? What am I doing to build a relationship with the Lord? Do I focus more on the "doing" or am I spending time with Him in thoughtful reflection and prayer?

# APPENDIX

## HELPFUL WEB SITES

www.messies.com: a site with lots of great organizing resources.

http://www.nsgcd.org: the home page of The National Study Group on Chronic Disorganization.

http://www.napo.net: for referrals to professional organizers.

http://www.faithfulorganizers.com: find a Christian professional organizer near you.

http://www.freecycle.org: an organization to help you get rid of the clutter by offering a venue in which you can give it away.

## RECOMMENDED READING

### De-Cluttering, Cleaning, and Organizing

Aslett, Don. *Clutter's Last Stand: It's Time to De-Junk Your Life!* 2005. This book was first released in 1984. Over 20 years later its timeless contents hit the bookshelves again. One of the best de-cluttering books I ever read.

Aslett, Don, and Laura Aslett Simons. *Make Your House Do the Housework.* 1995. A must-read for anyone who wants to learn how make to wise decorating and remodeling decisions. It teaches about low-maintenance and easy-to-clean window treatments, flooring, furniture, and other home treatments.

Cilley, Marla. *Sink Reflections: Overwhelmed? Disorganized? Living in Chaos? The FlyLady's Simple Flying Lessons Will Show You How to Get Your Home and Your Life in Order—and It All Starts with Shining Your Sink!* 2002. Weaved with wit and wisdom, this book offers great tips for individuals who struggle to keep a clean home.

Felton, Sandra. *Neat Mom, Messie Kids: A Survival Guide.* 2002. Written for the neat mom and the mom who wants to be neat. Learn how to hone the skills of a successful home manager by bringing your family together as a team to conquer housework.

———. *The New Messies Manual: The Procrastinator's Guide to Good Housekeeping.* 2000. This perennial charmer offers insights into the world of a messie with practical advice on how to clean and de-clutter.

Hemphill, Barbara. *Taming the Paper Tiger at Home.* 2005. A guidebook to organizing papers at home. Contains easy-to-follow, excellent tips.

Izsak, Barry. *Organize Your Garage in No Time.* 2005. Step-by-step instructions for organizing your garage.

Morgenstern, Julie. *Organizing from the Inside Out: The Foolproof System for Organizing Your Home, Your Office, and Your Life.* 2004. Once you get the clutter out, this resource is invaluable. Learn how to organize your rooms in a way that fends off clutter.

Peel, Kathy. *The Family Manager Takes Charge: Getting on the Fast Track to a Happy, Organized Home.* 2003. Lots of ideas and useful information. A great read.

Ramsland, Marcia. *Simplify Your Life: Get Organized and Stay That Way.* 2005. Refreshing new ways to simplify a busy life, paperwork at home and office/home office, as well as practical tips for keeping a peaceful home and life.

Salzmann, Cyndy. *Making Your Home a Haven: Strategies for the Domestically Challenged.* 2001. The author shares her own struggles with housekeeping and the solutions that worked for her. Includes a faith-based component.

## Family

Blanchard, Kenneth, et al. *Whale Done! The Power of Positive Relationships.* 2002. An easy-to-read book teaching the training methods used for killer whales and how these methods can be successfully used in nurturing relationships.

Cloud, Henry, and John Townsend. *Boundaries.* 2002. Learn how setting healthy boundaries will improve your life.

Covey, Stephen. *The Seven Habits of Highly Effective Families.* 1998. Dig deeper in how to create a family that works as a team. Learn how to write family mission statements.

Merrill, A. Roger, and Rebecca Merrill. *Life Matters: Creating a Dynamic Balance of Work, Family, Time, and Money.* 2003. Explores concepts like determining priorities, creating balance, and setting goals.

Swenson, Richard. *Margin: Restoring Emotional, Physical, Financial, and Time Reserves to Overloaded Lives.* 1995. Explore the concept of margin. Learn how adding margin makes us more content, energetic, and effective.

## Finances

Gibson, Roger. *First Comes Love, Then Comes Money: Basic Steps to Avoid the #1 Conflict in Marriage.* 1998. Explore working as a team in money management as husband and wife.

Hunt, Mary. *Mary Hunt's Debt-Proof Living: The Complete Guide to Living Financially Free.* 1999. Straight talk about how to live within your means and eliminate debt.

Ramsey, Dave, and Sharon Ramsey. *Financial Peace: Revisited.* 2002. One of the best resources to teach you a system to eliminate debt and build wealth.

Ramsey, Dave. *The Total Money Makeover: A Proven Plan for Financial Fitness.* 2003. The most motivational book on getting out of debt I've ever seen. Lots of practical information that can be immediately applied.

# NOTES

1. Carol Hamblet Adams, *My Beautiful Broken Shell* (Bloomington, Minn.: Garborg's, Inc., 1998).

2. Don Aslett, *Clutter's Last Stand: It's Time to De-Junk Your Life!* (Cincinnati: Writer's Digest Books, 1984), 3.

3. Kathy Peel, *The Family Manager's Everyday Survival Guide* (New York: Ballantine Books; 1st ed., 1998), 12.

4. Emilie Barnes, *Welcome Home* (Eugene, Oreg.: Harvest House, 1997), 11.

5. Pam Young and Peggy Jones, *Get Your Act Together: A 7-Day Get-Organized Program for the Overworked, Overbooked, and Overwhelmed* (New York: Harper Collins; 1st ed., 1993), 7.

6. Richard Swenson, *Margin/The Overload Syndrome: Learning to Live Within Your Limits* (Colorado Springs, Colo.: NavPress, 2002), 86.

7. Jeff Campbell, *Clutter Control: Putting Your Home on a Diet* (New York: Dell, 1992), 103.

8. Julie Morgenstern, *Organizing from the Inside Out* (New York: Henry Holt and Company, 1998), 191.

9. Cyndy Salzmann, *Making Your Home a Haven: Strategies for the Domestically Challenged* (Camp Hill, Pa.: Horizon, 2001), 84.

10. Kim Woodburn and Aggie MacKenzie, *How Clean Is Your House? Hundreds of Handy Tips to Make Your Home Sparkle* (New York: Dutton Books, 2004), 115.

11. Marla Cilley, *Sink Reflections: Overwhelmed? Disorganized? Living in Chaos? The FlyLady's Simple FLYing Lessons Will Show You How to Get Your Home and Your Life in Order—and It All Starts with Shining Your Sink!* (New York: Bantam, 2002), 168.

12. Barry Izsak, *Organize Your Garage . . . in No Time* (Indianapolis: Que, 2005), 32.

13. Deniece Schofield, *Confessions of a Happily Organized Family* (Cincinnati: Betterway Books, 1998), 74.

14. Barbara K. Mouser, *Five Aspects of a Woman* (Waxahachie, Tex., International Council for Gender Studies [ICGS]), 2002, 36.

15. Mary Hunt, *Mary Hunt's Debt-Proof Living: The Complete Guide to Living Financially Free* (Nashville: Broadman and Holman, 1999), 1.

16. Linda Cobb, *The Queen of Clean Conquers Clutter* (New York: Pocket Books, 2002), 22.

17. Barbara Hemphill, *Taming the Paper Tiger at Home* (Washington, D.C.: Kiplinger Books; 5th ed., 1998), xi.

18. Sandra Felton, *The New Messies Manual: The Procrastinator's Guide to Good Housekeeping* (Grand Rapids: Revell; 3rd ed., 2000), 41.